Your Towns and Cities in Wor

Cornwall

at War 1939-1945

Your Towns and Cities in World War Two

Cornwall
at War 1939-1945

By Derek Tait

First published in Great Britain in 2017 by
PEN & SWORD MILITARY
an imprint of
Pen and Sword Books Ltd
47 Church Street
Barnsley
South Yorkshire S70 2AS

ISBN 978 1 47389 2 248

Printed and bound in England
by CPI Group (UK) Ltd, Croydon, CR0 4YY

Pen & Sword Books Ltd incorporates the imprints of Pen & Sword
Archaeology, Atlas, Aviation, Battleground, Discovery, Family History,
History, Maritime, Military, Naval, Politics, Railways, Select, Social History,
Transport, True Crime, and Claymore Press, Frontline Books, Leo Cooper,
Praetorian Press, Remember When, Seaforth Publishing and Wharncliffe.

For a complete list of Pen and Sword titles please contact
Pen and Sword Books Limited
47 Church Street, Barnsley, South Yorkshire, S70 2AS, England
E-mail: enquiries@pen-and-sword.co.uk
Website: www.pen-and-sword.co.uk

Contents

CHAPTER ONE

1939 – The Outbreak of War

The rise of Adolf Hitler and the Nazi party together with tensions in Europe and the spread of fascism in other parts of Europe ultimately led to the start of the Second World War. When Germany invaded Poland on 1 September 1939, outrage was felt across the world. Great Britain and France declared war on Germany two days later.

Hitler seen at a captured Polish air base studying a map with General Von Reichenau.

The year before the war, Chamberlain travelled to Germany to appease Hitler. Pictured beside him is the German Foreign Minister Joachim von Ribbentrop. Hitler promised Ribbentrop St Michael's Mount should Germany win the war.

Lights all over Cornwall were turned off and a compulsory order was issued to prevent home owners from allowing any light to be seen from outside their premises. The order also applied to businesses and shop owners who had to turn off any illuminated signs as well as lights in their windows. Motorists were required to fit regulation masks to their headlights. With the general feeling that the conflict would escalate, there had already been a great demand for black-out material, so much so that shops soon ran out.

On 3 September, the Prime Minister, Neville Chamberlain, announced the outbreak of war on the radio.

The general mobilization of armed forces began and the National Services Act was passed by parliament introducing National Service for all men aged between 18 and 41.

An order was issued to stop people gathering in large crowds which meant that places of entertainment such as cinemas and theatres were closed. The few people who had television sets found that the BBC had stopped broadcasting for the duration of the war. Memories of the First World War were still fresh in the minds of many residents in Cornwall and most knew what to expect.

Four evacuated children taking it easy after the long train journey to Cornwall. Their belongings are all in haversacks or cases.

Neville Chamberlain announcing the outbreak of war on the BBC on 3 September 1939. The news was broadcast at 11.15 am.

A warning was issued which stated:

Keep yourself off the streets as much as possible; to expose yourself unnecessarily adds to your danger. Carry your gas mask with you always. Make sure every member of your household have on them their names and addresses clearly written. Do this on an envelope or luggage label and not on an odd piece of paper which may be lost. Sew a label on children's clothing so that they cannot pull it off. People are requested not to crowd together unnecessarily in any circumstances. Churches and other places of public worship will not be closed. All day schools in evacuation and neutral areas in England, Wales and Scotland are to be closed for lessons for at least a week.

During the beginning of September, about 2,000 women and children were evacuated to Cornwall. Lady Vivian, the chief of the Women's Auxiliary Service for Cornwall, was present at St Austell railway station to meet 544 schoolchildren and their teachers who had been evacuated from London. It was noted that the children looked very tired but cheerful. The only mother to accompany the children was Mrs Stephens, who was a caretaker at one of the schools. She brought with her seven of her children. One of the teachers said that the children behaved very well and that many of them thought that they were going

James B. Nicholson DSO, the Head Air Raid Warden, seen outside the Masonic Hall in Saltash on 7 June 1939. Gas masks were issued from the building. Regular drills were held in the town, especially for school children, to show them how the masks should be used in case of attack.

on holiday. They didn't eat much, apart from sweets, and few touched their rations. The older children knew the reason for the journey but the younger ones thought that they were going to pick blackberries.

From the train, the children marched to the huge Western National shed adjoining the station where Girl Guides and Boy Scouts handed out refreshments. Children were allocated their billets and a loud cheer went up when some of them realized that they were being sent to the seaside. The *West Briton and Cornwall Advertiser* reported that the scene at Truro Station was unforgettable as 230 mothers and children arrived from Acton to find new homes in the city. Girl Guides and Red Cross nurses assisted mothers with their young children and scouts helped carry their baggage. The Truro contingent marched to Bosvigo School where they were given refreshments, including tea and biscuits.

At Camborne, 960 evacuees from London were welcomed and found homes throughout the district. Hundreds of people gathered at the train station to witness their arrival. All the youngsters were carrying gas masks in cloth receptacles slung over their shoulders. They were taken to the Girls' County School where they were given refreshments before they were found new homes. Each carried a parcel of clothing and rations and had a label attached to them with their name and address.

Meanwhile in London, between two and three thousand American refugees left the city during the night. Many were destitute. An American Embassy official stated that it might take ten days before there would be sufficient ships to evacuate them all. Joseph Kennedy, the American Ambassador, appealed to all American and other neutral steamship companies to provide available ships, including freighters and tankers, to aid with the evacuation.

On 4 September, Mr Edgar Trounson, of the firm of S. and T. Trounson Ltd, wholesale grocers and corn merchants of Redruth, stated that there was a normal supply of everything in the country at a meeting of the council of Redruth Chamber of Commerce. He remarked that there would be no shortage of grocery supplies whatsoever and that there would be no abnormal rise in prices. He added that everything was coming under government control as quickly as possible and all supplies would be organised. He mentioned that no one need be worried lest they were going to be short of essential articles of food. 'As far as we can see, everybody will have what he and she requires and prices will be fixed. If only people will act sensibly and purchase their normal week to week requirements and remain calm, there will be no shortage,' he stated.

Discussing food prices during war time, Falmouth and District Trades Council decided to keep an eye on possible profiteering. Mr A. Napier, presiding, explained that a food control committee was being set up for the town. 'There has been a big demand for foodstuffs, but I would not say it has been unreasonable, said Mr W.A. Jennings, of Truro, to a reporter. 'Sugar is one of the main items demanded, candles, matches and tinned goods, such as fish, meat and fruits are other things on which there has been a heavy call. There is no suspicion at all of red-hot hoarding by anyone and it is quite clear that there are excellent food stocks in wholesale premises in Cornwall.'

The council of Redruth Chamber of Commerce resolved unanimously to recommend that traders close their establishments at 8.00 pm on the next two Saturdays, instead of at 9.00 pm, and to remain open on the other weekdays until the normal closing time.

The Cornish hospitals were very busy completing their preparations to meet war-time conditions. Sitting-up cases were evacuated from the Royal Cornwall Infirmary and private cars were used to take the patients to their homes. In charge of the operation were the Women's Voluntary Service. Urgent cases were still received at the hospital which was fully staffed. Ten thousand sand bags were utilized in protecting the Royal Cornwall Hospital and another twenty-two thousand were expected to be used to protect the whole building. Instead of sand, the bags were filled with earth which was taken from the allotments at the back of the new extensions. The 400 windows at the Infirmary were blacked out with Italian cloth, black paper or black paint.

At the St Austell Cottage Hospital, fifteen patients were moved by members of the Voluntary Aid Detachment while men of the English China Clay Company busily erected sandbags to protect the building from possible air raids. At Helston and District Cottage Hospital, 20,000 sandbags were put in place, filled from dumps at St Keverne Quarries. Lighting was completely obscured and many patients were sent home. At the Newquay and District Hospital, school children, visitors and City Council workmen all helped to erect sandbags around the buildings.

At the West Cornwall Hospital at Penzance, provision was made to accommodate 104 people in addition to the hospital's normal capacity

A female horse rider from Truro pauses to knit a few stitches of a scarf to send to a soldier overseas. Home knitters provided an essential service to soldiers serving their country far away from home.

Evacuees arriving in Cornwall during September 1939. They were accompanied by their mothers, together with babies, and are pictured at Camborne railway station.

A National Registration Identity Card. The National Registration Act was introduced on 5 September 1939.

Evacuee school girls having tea at Basset Road School before being taken to their accommodation nearby.

Five men are seen filling sandbags to protect a public building in Truro. The sandbags provided essential protection during enemy attacks.

Several Land Girls, complete with a dog, being trained to lift potatoes at Meadowside Farm, Quenchwell.

of 55. Extra medical supplies were laid in and there was a month's reserve of drugs and dressings.

Two thousand people took to the beach at Falmouth and men, women and children all helped to fill sandbags. An appeal had been made by the Executive Committee of the Falmouth and District Hospital for 500 workers to fill sandbags. Sand was taken from Gyllyngvase Beach and scores of people joined in the task. The filled bags were carried to the hospital on lorries owned by the Falmouth Transport Company.

On 5 September, the National Registration Act was introduced by an act of parliament stating that all residents of the UK would have to carry ID cards.

On Thursday, 7 September, the *Western Morning News* reported that there was a shortage of members in the Land Army and appealed for women to join:

> Already the great exodus from the land has begun. Men are leaving the fields to take up arms for their country. Now it behoves the women of the West to carry on in their stead. The Devon and Cornish Women's Land Army is recruiting so anxiously just now. So far, Devon and Cornish women have made poor response to the calls of the Land Army. As yet Devon has enrolled 380 members, Devon alone aims at securing 7,000 women and girls for land work. The host of evacuated strangers in the area are setting a shining example to those with whom they have come to live. Several have joined forces already with the Land Army. Like the rest, they enrol either at their local employment exchange or with the district representative of the Land Army.

On 16 September, petrol rationing was introduced. There were substantial supplies of the fuel in the country but in the national interest, it was felt that these must be put to the best use. It was announced that there would be no change in the price of petrol at least for fourteen days.

Sports of all kinds were affected during September and there were many abandonments. One headline read 'Shortage of players and bad weather.' It

A sandbag wall being built to protect the Royal Cornwall Infirmary in Truro.

Children of Bosvigo School in Truro hurrying from their classrooms to a nearby shelter. All were taking part in a drill to show them what to do in the event of an enemy gas attack.

went on to say: 'The international situation and heavy rain combined played havoc with sport in the Westcountry on Saturday and, except for the more important league matches, few football engagements were carried out, clubs finding it impossible to get together full teams.'

The government had forbidden all sports where crowds were likely to assemble and league football ceased. Although the day was set for the opening of the rugby season there were no matches played in the west, and Plymouth Albion abandoned their practice game owing to the shortage of players.

The *Cornishman* of Tuesday, 26 September carried a story under the headline 'German U-boat fetches rescue ship.' It read:

Another strange story of the sea was unfolded when Captain Hugh McMichael, Falmouth captain of the *British Influence* and his crew were landed on Friday by a lifeboat which had transferred them from the Norwegian vessel *Ida Bakke*. The *British Influence* was sunk by a German U-boat on Thursday but not before the commander of the latter had shown the utmost chivalry by seeing the crew of the doomed ship safely aboard

Children from the United Services Orphan Home for Girls in Devonport on their way to their new school in Newquay.

a Norwegian boat. His action brought cheers from the British seamen and the crew of the U-boat responded with cheers for their opponents. John Atkinson had a graphic story to unfold. He was on watch about noon when he saw a submarine rise to the surface. 'An order was given by the submarine commander to lower the boats,' he said. 'The submarine had by this time come alongside. The commander asked the crew if they had sufficient food, tobacco and clothing. He then said he was going to sink the ship. The submarine again came alongside the lifeboats, and the commander said a rescue ship was on the way. He fired three rockets in the air to attract the rescue ships.'

Mr Atkinson said that when the rescue ships did not seem to be appearing, the submarine commander told the crew to wait where they were and he would go and get the rescue ships. After some time the submarine returned with the Norwegian ship, which took the men on board. When the crew of the *British Influence* were on board the Norwegian vessel, they gave cheers for the submarine crew. The crew replied by giving three cheers for the *British Influence* crew. The submarine then submerged.

Dr Ivens Knowles, the acting county director, inspects a British Red Cross Detachment, Cornwall 34, at Porthgwidden, Feock.

The Emergency War budget was introduced by Sir John Simon on 27 September. As well as petrol rationing, a duty was placed on whisky which was expected to raise an extra £3,500,000 a year. The tobacco duty and sugar duty was also raised. The latter led to an increase in the price of jam, marmalade, tinned fruit, syrup and sweetened milk.

During September, it was announced that 6,366 women had enlisted, in the southwest region, for the Women's Voluntary Service for Civil Defence. The area included Devon, Cornwall, Somerset, Dorset, Gloucestershire and Wiltshire.

This brought the total recruitment for the year up to 32,182.

Identity cards were introduced on 30 September.

Towards the end of September, the police searched the Regal Cinema in Penzance and found two drums of petrol underneath a pile of wood covered by a curtain. At the Penzance Police Court, Gwyther Eastlake Prance, of the Gem Cinema Offices, Redruth, licensee of the cinema, was fined £2 and 5s. costs for having kept petroleum spirit in a vessel of capacity exceeding two gallons without having given previous notice in writing to the local authority. The chief constable said that the local authority had not been informed that any petroleum was being stored at the cinema and they would not have agreed to it. On 26 September, PCs Toms and Symons told the manager of the Regal, Mr Fisher, that they had reason to believe that there was petroleum there. Mr Fisher replied, 'There certainly is not,' and he gave permission for the premises to be searched. Beneath the cinema, in a boiler room, they found two five-gallon drums of petrol under a pile of wood, covered by a piece of curtain. Mr Fisher stated that he did not know that the petrol was there as he had only recently come to the cinema. Mr Eric Thomas represented the defendant, who pleaded guilty. The defendant was a victim of circumstances entirely beyond his control, said Mr Thomas. He had, with lots of other people, bought some petrol before petrol rationing had come in. The drums were put in the Regal car park and covered with earth. Later, one of the Regal employees admitted that, thinking Mr Prance was coming there the following day and might want it, he put the petrol in the boiler room to await Mr Prance's arrival. Prance, who lived in Plymouth and conducted his business from Redruth, had not the slightest knowledge that the petrol was in the boiler room. The boiler room was not part of the Regal Cinema building and there was no communication from it to the cinema.

Sea defences were erected all around the coast in case of an enemy invasion.

A group of young Militiamen who had been called up and were reporting for duty at their nearest barracks.

On 1 October, the call-up proclamation stated that all men aged 20 to 21 must register with the military authorities.

At the beginning of October, it was announced that nearly fifty members of the Territorial Army Nursing Service were engaged in work at a military hospital 'somewhere in the Westcountry'. They were reportedly delighted with their surroundings and had shown particular interest in the scenery of the district saying that the hospital was ideally situated. Recruiting for the service had taken place in peace time when the majority of nurses joined. The two matrons in charge had been taken on at the end of the First World War. The nurses were from all over England but the majority had come from Birmingham.

Members of a territorial unit preparing for combat. During 1939, members of the Regular Army, Territorials and Militia became a single entity - the British Army.

Students being trained for the Land Army by Miss Henderson at Penmount, Truro. They are shown on a local farm trying to coax a reluctant cow onto a lorry.

Women decorate St John's Church in Truro with flowers, fruit and vegetables in preparation for the harvest festival thanksgiving services.

The Penhale tug-of-war team who won the championship of the Mining Division at Hayle in October. In August, they had won the championship of Cornwall at an event held in Camborne. The eight members of the team were described as teetotal and five were non-smokers.

Members of the Women's Land Army busily ploughing the fields. Women played a vital role during the war and kept the country going while their men were away fighting.

The *West Briton and Cornwall Advertiser* of Thursday, 19 October featured a story under the headline 'Farmers concerned about scale of payment of Women's Land Army.' It read:

> Agriculturists in Cornwall, who have been contemplating utilizing female labour recruited by the Women's Land Army, are concerned about the question of payment for their services. The Women's Land Army stipulates that after a member has done one month's training, her remuneration should not be less than 28 shillings per week. This is likely to cause discontent on the part of women who are normally engaged on the land, their pay being fixed by the Agricultural Wages Act at 5d per hour, which works out at several shillings per week less than being demanded for the Women's Land Army. A similar position arises in connection with youths employed on the land, their rate of pay being 26s 6d per week between the ages of 19 and 20. It is argued that women and youths who have been working on the land for years are worth more to their employers than newly-trained members of the Women's Land Army and it is expected that there will have to be a revision of the pay for Land Army workers if their services are to be fully utilized. Farmers are considering whether they can get full value for the wages paid and there is a strong view that the rate has been fixed too high. We understand that representations are being made to the Ministry regarding the scale of pay laid down for Women Land Army workers, pointing out that it upsets the balance of the normal women land workers and youths. The discrepancy between the two scales is said to be bound to upset the smooth working of farms where workers of the different types are employed. In Cornwall there are about 200 volunteers for the Women's Land Army and many of these are being trained, 34 farmers having provided facilities for training. Up to the present, there has been no great demand for the services of women workers as there appears to be, in most cases, sufficient labour on farms to cope with the work that has to be done. It has been found from inquiries at Labour Exchanges in the county that a plentiful supply of semi-skilled men are available. It is expected, however, that a shortage of labour will be felt about February, and farmers are being advised to make arrangements

Geoffrey Briggs, of Newquay, who was a Hornets and Cornwall rugby player, is seen having his photograph taken by his new wife, Margaret Norris, after their wedding in St Columb during October 1939.

to obtain male or female substitutes for the men who are called up for service with the Forces.

On 21 October, registration began for men aged between 20 and 23 to be called up for National Service. People who were exempt from the act included the medically unfit, students, clergy, conscientious objectors and people working in reserved occupations such as farming, baking and engineering. The call-up had a severe effect on many firms and some small businesses had to close down.

The *West Briton and Cornwall Advertiser* of 26 October stated that

Front and back views of the British army's new battle dress.

there were few conscientious objectors in Cornwall. It reported that hundreds of young Cornishmen between the ages of 20 and 22 had presented themselves at the Labour Exchanges for registration under the National Service (Armed Forces) Act, 1939. The number of conscientious objectors was very small. At St Austell, one man who registered was a deaf and dumb farm worker bearing an Italian name. However, it was discovered that he had been born in Canada and, as an infant, with a label attached to his clothing, had been saved from a wreck off the Cornish coast and taken care of by foster-parents, with whom he was still living. The registration went off very smoothly in West Cornwall, where 190 men registered at Penzance, Hayle, St Ives, St Just and the Isles of Scilly. There was only one conscientious objector, a man from Hayle. Of the men registered, eighty were dealt with at the Penzance employment exchange, thirty-eight at Hayle, thirty-two at St Ives, thirty-five at St Just and five in the Isles of Scilly. No fewer than sixty-four expressed a preference for the air force and forty-four desired to join the navy. The air force was much favoured in Penzance, where thirty-two of the eighty registered wished to enter the service. All the young men seemed quite cheerful, they looked fit and, it was reported, none of them were disabled. It was believed there were no abstentions from registration, and of the unemployed registered, four were at Penzance, two at St Ives, one at Hayle and one at St Just. The fact that the number registered in the area was about eighty fewer than some anticipated showed that many in West Cornwall had already entered the services as volunteers. In St Austell town there were 120 men registered, of whom one was a conscientious objector. In the district, the number who registered was 265. Other registration figures in Cornwall included (the number of conscientious objectors is given in brackets): Truro, 75 (2); Falmouth, 99 (1); Helston, 44 (1); Redruth, 99 (1); Camborne, 90 (2); Newquay, 28 (0); Perranporth and St Agnes, 15 (0).

At the beginning of November, a woman appeared in court in Penzance. She stated that she had been followed and bought drinks by a German spy. She was charged before the Penzance borough magistrates with being drunk and disorderly in Market Jew Street, Penzance. The woman, Iris Gilbart, of Chyalso, Perranuthnoe pleaded not guilty but the bench found the case proven and fined her 10 shillings, or seven days' imprisonment if the money was not paid in fifteen days. Chief Constable R.C.M. Jenkins said that on the previous Thursday night, PC Toms saw the defendant lying between the outer and inner doors of the Railway Hotel, Penzance and, thinking she was ill, went to her assistance. The licensee opened the door, and together they lifted the defendant inside and the constable then saw that she was drunk. The defendant was asked where she had come from but would say nothing at all. Later, she said that she came from Marazion but when a taxicab was provided to get her there, she refused to go.

The Bishop of Truro unveiling a new ambulance at Hayle during November 1939. He is pictured with ambulance staff and prominent members of the community.

The constable then told her he would have to arrest her. At this, the defendant became disorderly and violent and the constable had to get the assistance of three other people to get her into a taxi to take her to the police station. She gave her name as Peggy Dixon.

On 2 November, it was reported that at a meeting of the Royal Cornwall Agricultural Association in Truro, it was decided to suspend activities for the duration of the war. Consequently, the proposed Royal Cornwall Show at Falmouth in 1940 would not be held. It was also decided to allocate a sum of £100 to be divided between the Red Cross and St John Ambulance Fund.

On Thursday, 2 November, the *Cornishman* reported that demand was returning for Cornish flowers. The article read:

Cornwall's flower trade, badly hit during the early days of the war, is steadily reviving. There is a bigger demand for flowers again and hundreds of boxes of bright - hued anemones are being sent daily to the big centres. Mr H.W. Abbiss, county horticultural superintendent for Cornwall, says: 'Flowers brighten the home and help to keep us cheerful and for that reason it is wrong to regard them as an unnecessary luxury in war-time. There is no truth in the talk about wholesale destruction of flower crops in Cornwall to make way for food crops. This is sheer nonsense, because it is too late to do anything this year and also the flower grower who has hundreds of pounds sunk in his flowers must realize on his crop if he is to be able to put down cereals and vegetables in the spring. The flower grower is endeavouring to carry on more or less normally. No restrictions have been imposed as yet. Next spring, hundreds of acres now under use for flowers will be utilized for growing vegetables. This is why we should enjoy our flowers during the coming months, for they will not be so plentiful again until after the war is over.'

Miss R.S.M. Collett, of Truro, a well-known fruit and flower grower, said: 'There is a growing demand for flowers and we are sending to Covent Garden again. Birmingham has been the best market since war broke out.'

In the third week of November, the *Cornishman* recorded the views of local people on German broadcasts. The article read:

A number of people in West Cornwall have expressed their views on the value of the German broadcasts. Mr A.T. Holman, president of Camborne Division Conservative Association, considered the German news a vicious mixture of lies, threats,

Pupils of Truro County School for girls who had volunteered for the Cadet Detachment of the St John's Ambulance Brigade which was being formed in the city. Mrs A. Goode can be seen explaining the symbolism of the badge.

boasts and half truths. 'If we are induced by curiosity to listen to the broadcasts these undoubted facts should be kept firmly before us. For our own peace of mind, it is probably better to avoid such insidious propaganda and switch to neutral countries if we desire the independent view.'

Mr C.L. Rosewarne, chairman of Camborne Conservative Association, stated, 'In my opinion it depends on who the people are who listen. I find most of my friends listen to it as a matter of amusement. Generally speaking, I am of the opinion that it is just as well that they should listen to it. Its influence is exactly the opposite intended by the German propagandists. The more it is got abroad that we are taking it as a huge joke the better.'

The Mayor of Helston, Reverend E.J. Chappell, said, 'For the official or person who can test the accuracy of the statements, there is no harm done in listening to the German transmission in English. They are so grossly insulting and inaccurate, however, that it is perhaps better to leave them alone.'

Mr W.H. Lane, ex-mayor of Penzance, is of the opinion the only effect the Nazi radio propaganda has on listeners in this country is that the 'present leaders in Germany were unblushing liars.'

'It is regarded as harmless entertainment and is somewhat akin to the tub-thumping methods adopted by unscrupulous political partisans in the fever heat of an election who do not care what they say so long as their allegations are not denied on the spot. The continuance of the propaganda is only causing greater revulsion of feeling than previously existed. Personally, I prefer to go to bed thankful that I am not a German.'

Mr F.S. Shaw, chairman of the Watch Committee, Penzance, says, 'I have listened to some of these broadcasts myself. They are all abuse and no news. They have toned down a good deal since the beginning of the war and I don't listen to them now as much as I did at the outset. I don't think any harm will come listening to these talks. A person of average intelligence is not likely to be deceived by them. Most people regard them as good entertainment.'

Mr E.G. Pentreath, MC, a prominent member of the British

Legion and a member of Penzance Town Council, observed, 'I think we can assess their true value. I think the members of HM forces would prefer to hear the sports results from home. Those who know the Hun have their opinions confirmed as to his character and failure to understand other nations. The broadcasts lose the value they might have had to the Germans by their personal bitterness and inaccuracy.'

On Thursday, 23 November, the *Western Morning News* reported that a man had maimed his own hand to avoid army service.

Spectators at Penzance Quarter Sessions applauded when Norman Richards, aged 15, of Trevorian, Camborne, was convicted of having cut off two fingers from his right hand to avoid military service. He received a special recommendation for leniency from the jury and was bound over for three years. Richards said in the

A female member of the Civil Air Guard, part of the Home Front.

Women in uniform including members of the ATS, WRNS, WAAF, the Ambulance Corps and the Women's Land Army.

box that he was so terrified of stories of war horrors that he could not sleep. He was willing to serve his country at home but he could not fight 'nohow'.

The Recorder, Mr William Delamotte Mathias, told the accused, 'You have done an extremely stupid and wicked thing There is no doubt that for a very long time you have been very much worried but must remember that everybody in this country is worried to some extent.'

The *Western Morning News* of Monday, 4 December stated that it was Christmas as usual in the west. Many hotels in Devon and Cornwall remained open. It continued:

This will be Christmas as usual in most hotels throughout Devon and Cornwall. Far from the war keeping people at home and knocking the bottom out of the Christmas hotel trade, the opposite effect has been created. Distance from the theatre of war, immunity from air raids and the climatic

Men of the new army carrying out searchlight work in Cornwall.

Yuletide reputation of Cornwall and Devon have been important factors. There may be a black-out but that applies to all of Britain. All things considered, Christmas 1939 looks like creating a busy and prosperous season for the Westcountry hotelier. Not even petrol rationing will shake the determination of many to get what break they can from the monotonous boredom of the war. Railway companies have promised extra trains, too. Rationing will not be in force until after the festival. This has convinced many to enjoy to the utmost what will probably be the last unrationed Christmas of the war. Inquiries by *Western Morning News* reporters last week showed that Westcountry hotel managers have planned for a busy period.

The West's sheltered coastline and its comparative immunity from air raids are additional temptations to many people to choose it for a long Christmas holiday this year. For this reason it is expected that there will be a fair proportion of visitors to most Cornish resorts.

During the second week of December, it was announced that there had been an excellent response throughout the Camborne and Redruth urban district to the appeal for funds for the provision of Christmas parcels for all men and women from the district who were serving with the Forces. At Camborne, where Captain B. Kelly was the chairman of the committee, £42 had been received and further amounts were anticipated. Each of the 340 persons from the ward who were serving would all receive a tin of cigarettes valued at 3 shillings. Orders had already been placed for 115 tins to be sent direct by the manufacturers to men from the ward serving overseas and in the navy.

The response from residents of Redruth ward was particularly generous and over £70 had been collected. There were about 220 men and women from the ward serving with the Forces. Eighty parcels containing a writing pad, two pencils, a pack of playing cards, a bar of soap, fifty cigarettes and half a pound of chocolate, to a total value of 6 shillings, was dispatched to the men serving overseas. In a number of cases of men serving on ships, pipes were sent. The men and women serving within the country received a slightly smaller parcel, valued at 5 shillings.

Land Girls being put to the test. Mr H.W. Abbis, the county horticultural superintendent, can be seen putting several Land Girls through their examination at Miss R. Collett's farm at Perranwell.

By collecting 14 tonnes of old metal, ...ads at Heamoor, Penzance, were able ...o distribute parcels of Christmas goods ...o soldiers' wives over the festive season. A further £20 was sent as a gift to the ...overnment.

A Christmas party at Redruth. Mothers and their children attend a Redruth Infant Welfare Christmas party during December 1939.

In the Illogan Ward, the response was also very generous, with £70 having been collected. There were nearly 200 men from the ward on service and each received a similar parcel to those sent from Redruth.

The *West Briton and Cornwall Advertiser* of Monday, 25 December reported that there was a big shopping rush at Falmouth and that festive spirit continued in spite of the troubled times. The article read:

'Tis a bonny dee,' said a Scots patient from his bed in the Royal Cornwall Sailors' Hospital. And with this piece of typically native terseness, he unwittingly summarized the opinions of everybody about the Christmastide in Falmouth. Despite the stress of troublous times, the season lost none of those characteristics which have kept it alive throughout the centuries. In homes and institutions where the Message of Empire and the King's broadcast were heard over the wireless, the spirit was probably heightened and more so where families were depleted because of that now familiar factor, active service. In homes and in the larger family gatherings of the various institutions, Christmas Day pursued its normal, quiet course. There were services in the churches and carol singing. This, however, was preceded by one of the biggest shopping rushes on record, attributable, perhaps, to the intention to have a good time while possible and to the endeavours of housewives to secure reasonable luxuries before rationing begins.

Amid the bustle of mid-day shopping on Saturday, a party of singers from the Falmouth docks made the customary tour through the main street, singing carols and collecting for sick and needy workmates and their relatives. The party was organized by Mr H. Owen, the well-known bass singer, and Messrs S. Muller and H. Richardson were honorary secretaries. Also following custom, Falmouth Parish Church Choir visited Falmouth and District Hospital on Christmas Eve, singing carols to the patients in the wards, and on Christmas morning, Falmouth Town Band played in the hospital grounds. The hospital wards and corridors had been gaily bedecked by the staff, assisted by Mr J.H. Scoble (Penryn) and other helpers. Mr G.R. Green (chairman of the executive committee), Mrs Green and family and the mayor and mayoress (Mr and Mrs R.E. Gill) were among those who visited the patients during the morning. Well cared for by the Matron (Miss M. Forster), and the staff, the patients had as enjoyable a time as possible, and after the Christmas dinner, they were permitted to entertain two guests each in the afternoon and to tea, and later in the evening the nursing staff had a party in the nurses' hostel. The kitchen staff dinner was held on Tuesday. There is to be a party for in-patients, though, owing to the black-out, outpatients and former patients are not being invited, a disappointment for the many children who usually anticipate this.

CHAPTER TWO

1940 – The Battle of Britain

On 1 January, two million men aged between 19 and 27 were called up for military service in Great Britain.

In the first week in January, the *Western Morning News* carried an article stating that 'Comforts are really necessary.' It reported that after shutting for Christmas, Cornwall Central Hospital Supply Service had now reopened, receiving a steady stream of finished garments and comforts. The depot was organized by the British Red Cross, the Order of St John and the Women's Voluntary Service, who all worked happily together for the good cause, pooling their organizations' efforts and results.

Cornwall's 6,000 women workers had made 1,000 nightshirts and were now embarking on as many or more shirts. The committee felt that they were rightly interpreting the wishes of their supporters in sending the first fruits of Cornish produce to Cornishmen. Parcels were sent from the depot to the county regiment (through Mrs Mercer's depot at Bodmin), to other units and companies working in the county; to ships directly linked with Cornwall; to RAF men working in the West and to torpedoed and shipwrecked mariners landed at Western ports.

Because of Cornwall's huge coastline and in anticipation of an enemy invasion, the area was protected by gun emplacements, pill boxes and barbed wire. Road blocks were put in place and anti-tank obstacles erected at exits to beaches.

During 1940, RNAS St Merryn was rebuilt as a Fleet Air Arm Station and developed into a training base for airborne observers and aircraft carrier fighters.

The *Western Morning News* of Friday, 5

Members of the ATS search the skies for enemy bombers.

January, reported on the shortage of Anderson Shelters in Torpoint. It stated that Torpoint Urban Council were to make inquiries about Anderson steel shelters for 400 people which they had ordered during the previous July but which had so far not been delivered. At the Council's meeting on the previous night, Mr D.B. Peacock, chairman of the Highways Lighting and General Purposes Committee, suggested that a formal request for the shelters should be conveyed to the Cornwall County Council clerk, who would then take the matter up with the Home Office. 'We went to the Home Office about them as far back as July,' he said, 'and we have since tried to get delivery of them expedited. A railway official told me about a month ago that they were on their way but so far we have seen nothing of them. We might go on like this for months and as it is the Council's responsibility, we are not unnaturally a bit anxious.'

A shopkeeper detaches coupons from a ration book. The rationing scheme came into effect on 8 January 1940.

Mr Peacock's suggestion was adopted and it was also agreed to approach the County Council clerk with the suggestion that keys enclosed in glass panels should be installed near the public air-raid shelters. Mr Peacock instanced the experience of Plymouth, where it had been found that where the public shelters were open, fittings had been pilfered and the public had generally tampered with the Council's property. 'While we want to prevent that,' he said, 'it is manifestly ridiculous to spend some thousands on these shelters and then lock them and have people hanging about waiting for the key when they might want to use them urgently.'

On 8 January, sugar, bacon and butter were all rationed. Other essentials such as meat, tea, biscuits, jam, cheese, eggs, lard, milk, breakfast cereals as well as canned and dried fruit were also subsequently rationed.

Before the war, 55 million tons of food was imported into Britain from other countries. After 1939, the government had to restrict the amount of food coming into the country because the British supply ships were being attacked by German submarines. Rationing of food lasted until July 1954.

On 17 January, a spell of freezing weather hit the country causing the River Thames to freeze.

The *Western Morning News* of Wednesday, 31 January reported on a strange apathy towards making comforts at Millbrook. It said that from all quarters of Devon and Cornwall, they had published reports showing the enthusiasm with which towns and hamlets were providing comforts for Service men. Yet at Millbrook, a Cornish village nestling in a creek of the Tamar running up from Devonport Dockyard, itself a home of Service folk, little was being done. Although the population reached nearly 1,900 and consisted largely of ex-Service men, their families and Dockyard workers, there was no organized league, nor sewing parties. The *Western Morning News* stated that this was probably due to lack of leadership rather than from any want of patriotism, it continued that usually, when anything was needed, there was a ready response from the villagers. Although nothing was being done collectively, there were small numbers attending organizations at Cawsand and working there weekly. They also brought home wool and distributed it. When the articles were finished they took them back. During the last war, Millbrook had played a leading part in the West in this respect, but those who participated then were now twenty-five years older. Soon after the outbreak of the last war, a Patriotic League was formed, with the late Lady Ernestine Edgcumbe as president and Miss C.V. F. Little as secretary. Its objective was to respond to any call from King and Country.

By 1940, agriculture had lost 30,000 men to the British army and another 15,000 to other vital work. The severe shortage of labour prompted the government to form the Land Army. By 1944, there were over 80,000 women working on the land doing anything from milking and general farm work to cutting down trees and working in saw mills.

The Agriculture Committee, realized the devastation caused by rabbits, and urged farmers to shoot them. Rabbit was in demand and was much sought after by housewives, as well as chefs and hotels, who were all living with rationing.

Farms which kept over fifty hens had to send all their eggs to the

Women of the Land Army learning how to thatch a roof. The work was long and laborious and took a lot of skill to complete properly.

Land Army girls pointing stakes for fencing.

The Land Army girls packing sugar beet tops into a silo.

Ministry. For this reason, many farmers ensured that they only had forty nine.

The *Cornishman* of Thursday, 1 February, told of a fishing vessel at Newlyn which had been machine-gunned by German planes. It reported that marks of her ordeal could still be seen on the deck and in the bulwarks. The skipper told a remarkable story. He said that one night, he was returning to port when he heard planes roaring overhead. He took no notice of them, he thought they were friendly planes on convoy duty. Suddenly, one appeared out of the dark, flashing signals which the skipper took to be Morse to the convoy ships. The plane was not much higher than the mast head. All of a sudden, there was a splutter of machine gun bullets all along the deck. These bullets went right through the deck and some of them came through the bulk-head of the boat. Fortunately, none of the crew was injured. The planes then flew off and the vessel returned to port. Some of the bullets remained in the deck and sides of the boat.

The *Cornishman* of Thursday, 22 February, told how Cornish farmers were 'prepared to do their bit.' They reported that, speaking at the annual meeting of St Columb's Farmers' Union, on the previous Monday, Mr F.A. Trewhella, of Camborne, chairman of Cornwall Farmers' Union, remarked that as farmers they were asked to do their bit in maintaining what was known as the Home Front, and 'we are prepared to do that,' he said. 'We are prepared to put our backs into it and do all we possibly can but at the same time want a fair and square deal.' Speaking of the machinery which had been set up to secure an increase in arable farming, Mr Trewhella said:

Here in Cornwall, the response has been great and I believe everyone will cultivate the required acreage, although there may be one or two stubborn exceptions. The government were all out for increased arable production and livestock had to take second place. Some of them had been rather critical of the government's policy concerning livestock and the criticism had been well founded because the government knew before war broke out what their policy was, but farmers were kept in the dark. They were told there were adequate stocks for pigs and poultry, but they had a rude awakening and were left to get rid of their livestock as best they could. The number of pigs in this country was much higher than 1914 and the same applied to poultry, and it seemed, according to the policy of the government, they must be decreased. The Minister of Agriculture had not said in so many words, but when he expected producers to carry on with the feeding of their pigs and poultry with at least a third less feeding-stuffs, it was quite plain that they must reduce their number.

He urged that farmers should know what they were to receive for their advance, the same way as applied to munitions and other industries. They did not ask for unreasonable profits and were not profiteers but they did ask for some return for their work.

The *Western Morning News* of Saturday, 24 February, reported on the organization of salvage:

How is the Salvage Depot of the Ministry of Supply operating? How many Councils and business houses throughout the country are procrastinating? It is certainly fact that all over the country, to say nothing of Devon and Cornwall, there are householders who are unable to find anyone to collect their waste paper. Can it be that the spirit of leadership is lacking through the absence of the younger generation that has been called on to join the armed forces of the Crown? The *Western Morning News*, on making an inquiry in Bodmin yesterday, was told that the Corporation so far had not made any definite arrangements themselves for the salvage of waste paper and other waste products, for which the Salvage Department of the Ministry of Supply is clamouring. The Town Council is assisting the local organizations such as those worked by the Boy Scouts and other voluntary workers, in their task. Promises of help are being sought and the refuse collectors are being asked to help in the collection of waste paper and other salvable articles required by the Ministry. It is quite possible that householders will be reminded of the part that they can play in the nation's effort to avoid waste by the issue of handbills. At any rate, the matter has been under consideration.

Wadebridge Rural District Council, whose authority includes the area once controlled by the former Bodmin District Council, has given consideration to various suggestions for schemes for salvage of waste paper, bottles, old iron and other materials.

The 1st Cornwall Company of the ATS being inspected by the Company Commander, Mrs D. Blair.

Clerical staff of the ATS busily doing office work for the army.

A female member of the ATS storing rifles and other essentials ready for use by local regiments.

The Cornish girls of the ATS, who also worked as cooks, had to rise at 5.00 am on alternate mornings to provide meals for the troops.

Members of the ATS being inspected during a dress parade.

A sergeant in the ATS supervising the cooking of meals for the troops.

Cooks of the ATS preparing potatoes.

ATS storekeepers of the 1st Cornwall Company stacking the day's supply of bread.

In the different parishes in which the refuse is being collected, it is proposed to arrange for the salvaged goods to be conveyed to a covered depot, whence it will be collected at regular intervals, the central station being Wadebridge. Thence the salvage will be dispatched to the different centres nominated by the Ministry of Supply. In the bigger places, Boy Scouts have been active for a long time but in the isolated areas, there is a need for organization, although this is at hand. Liskeard Town Council, so far has not approved a programme of salvage work in the township. At the last meeting there was a discussion on the topic and a recommendation that no action should be taken was referred back to the Highways Committee.

The *Western Morning News* of Saturday, 23 March, reported that Cornish pasties were definitely not to be rationed. They stated that whatever the meat content, sausages, sausage meat, meat pasties, meat puddings and all other manufactured meat products would be sold free of the ration from the following Tuesday, after an announcement by the Ministry of Food. Issue of extra meat rations to diabetic patients was now authorized. Diabetics could obtain, in exchange for their sugar ration, an additional allowance of meat to the value of 1s 10d a week for adults and of 11d a week for children under six. Devon and Cornwall Food Control Offices had a busy time on the previous Thursday with people asking for emergency cards. Emergency ration books, which enabled the holder to purchase rationed foods at any shops, instead of those where he or she was registered, could be obtained either in one's home town before leaving for a holiday or business trip, or at one's destination, whichever was the more convenient. The following week, housewives saw one of their rationing problems overcome, when the butter ration per head was doubled from four ounces to eight ounces. Most Westcountry folk were accustomed to eating a fair amount of butter and the small ration had resulted in frequent laments.

On Saturday, 13 April, an official notification was given that the

Paper Controller had reduced the ration of paper from 60 per cent of pre-war consumption to 30 per cent. So drastic was the curtailment of the raw material that it greatly affected the newspaper industry.

The *Cornishman* of Thursday, 18 April, carried a story about the position of the mines in Cornwall during war-time. They stated that the special correspondent of *The Times* had said that industrial Cornwall was mostly forgotten by people living outside the Duchy who recalled only the enchanting coves on its long coastline. Yet tin was being obtained in the county nearly 3,000 years ago and, by the middle of last century, the mines of Cornwall were producing three-quarters of all the copper used in the world and nearly half the tin. But the industry fell away and today the tin area was scarred with the derelict buildings of disused mines. The reason was that while Malayan tin could be picked up on the surface for £30 a ton, it cost £140 to £150 to dig deep into the earth to obtain a ton of Cornish tin. A shaft might go down as much 2,000ft, and water must be kept out, resulting in heavy pumping charges.

With interference with shipments from abroad showing a marked rise, price would increase the demand for Cornish tin. Whether that demand could be met was another question. Already the industry was experiencing a scarcity of skilled labour. The position could be eased by making underground tin mining a totally reserved occupation and, as it was at present reserved at 23, the Forces would lose little in man-power. Trained miners were irreplaceable and it was claimed that men and youths who from the age of 16 had been trained for four or five years in modern mechanical methods underground could be of more service to their country in the mine than in the army.

'There are some old miners,' stated Mr C.V. Paull, a leading man in the industry and captain of the county cricket side, 'who worked in mines which were now closed and who were suffering to a greater or less degree from silicosis, and the financial burden which might arise from employing these men is too great for the mines to carry.'

The labour problem was increased by the fact that youths were drawn from the industry by the high wages to be had as labourers on government contract work. Other war-time difficulties were increased costs (on timber, steel, machinery and wages and later possibly a scarcity of timber). Financially the industry was in about the same position as before the war, for the price of the commodity had gone up about the same amount as costs had risen. Where thousands used to be employed, there were perhaps 1,200 men left in the industry, of whom well over half were underground workers.

On 23 April, purchase tax and an increased duty on tobacco were introduced as part of the War Budget. Income tax went up and beer was raised by 1d a pint. Whisky, tobacco and postal charges were all raised and it was hoped that the budget would raise £1,234,000,000 towards

A Cornish plum orchard in bloom at Coombe, near Truro, during April 1940.

the estimated expenditure for the year of £2,667,000,000.

On 10 May, Neville Chamberlain resigned as Prime Minister. Winston Churchill took his place.

On 14 May, recruitment commenced for the Local Defence Volunteers. They would later be renamed the Home Guard.

On 16 May, the internment of aliens living in the country began on a large scale.

Between 26 May and 4 June, the evacuation of the British Expeditionary Force at Dunkirk took place. Over 300,000 troops were rescued and returned to England. All types of boats, many from Cornwall, took part in the rescue including fishing vessels, pleasure boats, lifeboats and merchant marine boats. The flotilla of small boats undoubtedly saved thousands of lives.

Winston Churchill who replaced Neville Chamberlain as Prime Minister during 1940. He is pictured wearing a steel helmet during an air raid warning in 1940.

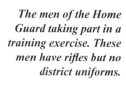

The men of the Home Guard taking part in a training exercise. These men have rifles but no district uniforms.

Some of the members of the Cornwall Women's Land Army who paraded through the streets of Truro during May.

The *Cornishman* of Thursday, 30 May, reported that there had been a rush to join the St Ives Local Defence Volunteers. At a crowded meeting at St Ives, on the previous Tuesday evening, addressed by Major Watson Smyth, the divisional commander of the LDV, said that the action of the King of the Belgians in throwing in his hand had put the BEF in an extremely grave situation. 'But,' he added, 'any of you who have had anything to do with our present army know quite well that the army is not going to give in, no matter what the odds against it are. Times are grave now and they possibly will be graver. One of the duties for which this force is formed, quite apart from parashooting,' he said, 'is to keep up the morale of the civilian population and

An appeal for young men to join the Home Defence.

I trust every member who enrols in this force will remember that this is one of his principal duties. Discount all rumours and never believe anything unless you hear it on the wireless or read it in your paper.'

Their duty was to observe and, if possible, to hold up the enemy for as long as they could with the arms at their disposal.

During May and June 1940, Germany invaded France, arriving in Paris on 14 June. By occupying France, the Germans were in a better strategic position to start bombing Great Britain.

Winston Churchill discussing the progress of the war.

On the 4 June, Winston Churchill made his famous 'We will fight them on the beaches' speech in the House of Commons.

The *Cornishman* of Thursday, 6 June, reported on air-raid warning sounds at Penzance saying that the practice should not have taken place. It stated that in the columns of the paper on the previous Saturday, there appeared a notice to the effect that in future the monthly practice of air-raid warnings at Penzance would not be sounded. This was highly advisable, since, now that the danger of an enemy attack loomed ever nearer, a practice warning would only serve to confuse the public, who, if an actual raid did ever occur on the first Monday in the month, would have merely regarded the siren as having been another test.

However, people were surprised when, at a police station to discover the reason for this extraordinary state of affairs, they were met with the reply that there had been a misunderstanding.

During June, St Catherine's Castle, which was originally built by Henry VIII, became an observation post. A gun battery was later added with two guns.

In June 1940, during the Battle of Britain, RAF St Eval became a fighter command headquarters housing Supermarine Spitfires as well as Hawker Hurricane and Bristol Blenheim fighters.

St Eval provided anti-submarine and anti-shipping patrols along the south west coast. Aircraft stationed there were also responsible for photographic reconnaissance missions, meteorological flights, air-sea rescue, convoy patrols and defence against the Luftwaffe.

The airfield came under attack several times in the summer of 1940 and early 1941 causing considerable damage.

The *Western Morning News* of Monday, 10 June, reported that most of the new evacuees were heading west. Many school children were due to leave Greater London. The evacuation was announced on the previous night and started on the following Thursday morning. It involved about 120,000 children, the majority of whom were to travel to Cornwall, Devonshire, Somerset and Wales. None would be sent to the Eastern Counties. The great exodus, which involved only those children who were registered, took six days to complete. The Ministry of Health statement on the evacuation under the registration scheme stated: 'In view of recent developments in the war and of the

Women of the ATS unloading Winchester rifles for use by members of the army.

commencement of enemy bombing of England, the Government do not feel right that this movement should be delayed any longer.'

It was added that the numbers to be sent to receiving districts would not exceed those allotted to them. The government recognized that the reception of the children would involve trouble to the authorities and householders in receiving districts but they knew that at this time of national emergency, the nation could rely on their support in the measures which were being taken to protect the lives of the children and to ease the problems of national defence. The position in all the evacuation areas would continue to be kept under daily review.

Children are shown how to put on and use their gas masks properly by their teacher. Regular drills took place at schools in Cornwall.

On 10 June, Italy declared war on France and Great Britain.

On 17 June, RMS *Lancastria* was destroyed by the Luftwaffe while evacuating British troops and nationals from Saint-Nazaire with the loss of 4,000 lives.

The first German bombs fell on Cornwall on 29 June and landed at Torpoint. At one o'clock, two high explosive bombs fell at Merrifield. There were no damage or casualties.

On 30 June, the German forces occupied Guernsey.

The *Cornishman* of Thursday, 4 July, carried a story about Cornwall's 4,000 unemployed. It mentioned that at a meeting of the Cornwall Highways Committee at Truro, on the previous Friday, Mr W.J. Orchard mentioned that there were 4,000 unemployed in the county. He mentioned that the 4,000 might have decreased through recent reshuffling. The Surveyor stated that 880 fewer men were employed and 440 of those had been engaged on maintenance work. The County Surveyor gave a summary of expenditure for the year, showing that the net was £374,435, as compared with the estimate of

£397,677. The reason for under-expenditure was the cutting down of work owing to the outbreak of war.

On 9 July, the Battle of Britain began.

On 12 July, RAF St Eval came under attack. Eight bombs were dropped by a Ju 88. The bombs caused minor damage and the German plane was seen off by two Spitfires.

The *Western Morning News* of Friday, 19 July, told that the proudest woman in Britain was Mrs Jessie Pearson, of Trowan Vean, St Ives. Her daughter, Corporal (now Assistant Section Leader) Joan Daphne Mary Pearson, had been recommended for the OBE. It was stated that this would be the first award of the war to a member of the WAAF.

An RAF list of awards published the day before described how Miss Pearson had saved a pilot's

A poster appealing for women to join the ATS.

life by pulling him from a burning plane and then throwing herself on top of him when one of the bombs on board exploded. Aged 29, Miss Pearson joined the WAAF in Kent in April, 1939, reaching her present rank in June of 1940. She was well known in St Ives, where for some years she was the proprietress of a photographic studio. Mrs Pearson told the *Western Morning News* that her daughter had written some time ago and said: 'I hear they are going to submit my name to the King, but I hope they won't, for when I hear what the boys have done at Dunkirk I know my little bit was nothing.'

Miss Pearson's father was Reverend J.H. Pearson, the vicar of Coombe, Oxford, who had died in December, 1932. Her ambition was to be a pilot but war broke out just before she got her certificate. She was determined to do war service, however, and applied to join the transport section as she was able to drive a car. There were no vacancies and she was asked if she would do medical work. She agreed and became the first woman medical orderly. The official account of her bravery said:

> On May 31, 1940, at 1 am, an aircraft crashed near the Women's Auxiliary Air Force quarters, the pilot being seriously injured.

Upon hearing the crash, Corporal Pearson rushed out to it and although the aircraft was burning and she knew that there were bombs aboard, she stood on the wreckage, roused the pilot, who was stunned, and assisted him in getting clear, releasing his parachute harness in doing so.

When he was on the ground, a 120lb bomb went off. Corporal Pearson at once threw herself on top of the pilot to protect him from the blast and splinters. Her prompt and courageous action undoubtedly helped to save the pilot's life.

During the summer of 1940, with fears of an imminent invasion, RAF's Coastal Command sent patrols to the coastline every day to check for signs of any enemy landings.

The *Western Morning News* of Monday, 5 August, carried a story under the headline, 'Help to down Hitler.' It stated that Mr J. Kerr, a barrister, was voluntarily undertaking a campaign with a cinema van on behalf of the National Savings effort and was now touring the towns and villages of Cornwall. On the previous Saturday, he had visited Newlyn East, Zelah, Chacewater, Devoran and Feock and later visited Tregony, Probus and Truro.

At Chacewater, Mr Kerr urged that the only way to get out of the war was to dig down. They had to set themselves to work for victory as hard as they could and the sooner they got it done, the sooner there would be peace. He added that we were the only nation left to fight the battle for freedom and even the little children were helping by saving through their school groups.

On 9 August, Birmingham was badly bombed.

In parliament on 20 August, Winston Churchill paid tribute to the RAF when he stated, 'Never in the field of human conflict was so much owed by so many to so few.'

On 21 August, RAF St Eval was bombed by three Ju 88s which caused damage to two hangars resulting in the destruction of three Blenheims. Hurricanes chased the raiders and shot down two of their aircraft. On the following day, 200 incendiaries and 14 high explosive bombs were dropped on the base but caused little damage.

On 23 August, a bomb hit a pyrotechnics store at St Eval which caused a huge explosion. The base was further bombed on 26 August between the hours of 21.30 and 21.58 pm.

The *Cornishman* of Thursday, 22 August, featured a story under the headline 'Scillonian's magnificent gift. Mr Birkinshaw gives a Spitfire.' The story told how Mr W.S.K. Birkinshaw, of Seaways, St Mary's, Isles of Scilly, had given a Spitfire to the nation, to be called the 'Scillonian'. This was not the first time that Mr Birkinshaw has shown practical munificence at Scilly. Previously, he had built the Isles of Scilly Hospital at Penninie, St Mary's, and had given it to the Islands.

On 24 August, the first air raid took place on London. Britain bombed Berlin for the first time on 26 August.

The *Western Morning News* of Friday, 30 August, reported on bombing raids in the Isles of Scilly. It stated that there had been air raids by Nazi planes on several days. Only on two occasions were the raids made by a solitary bomber. On other days, there had been two and three bombers over the islands. During these raids, over 100 high explosive bombs had been dropped. In addition, there had been many incendiary bombs. A number of the high-explosives found their mark. Casualties had been few. On each occasion the Germans had deliberately machine-gunned the island. Miss Groves, daughter of a coastguard, was killed by a bullet while in a shelter. German planes dived low over one the islands of Scilly the previous afternoon and systematically machine-gunned the islands. Rapidly, the residents dove for what shelter they could find and in consequence there were only two casualties, these slight. In addition, dozens of incendiary bombs were scattered throughout the island and a number of small fires started.

Some feeling existed about the lack of the provision of proper air-raid shelters in the area.

The *Western Morning News* stated that it understood that some difficulty was found in dealing with outbreaks of fire, the only appliances being stirrup-pumps. Following representations, extra apparatus for fire-fighting had been sent to the islands from the mainland. There was much jubilation at the arrival of the first trailer-pump. In view of the fact of the isolation the islands and the fact that they could not call on surrounding districts like a place on the mainland could if attacked, it was probable that the whole of the ARP in the islands would receive further consideration and possible attention.

At the beginning of September, the *Cornishman* mentioned the visit of Alec Beechman, MP, to the Isles of Scilly. It stated:

To the Nazi bombed and machine-gunned Isles of Scilly sailed, this Saturday morning, Mr Alec Beechman, MP, in whose constituency these islands lie. He wants to go and see for himself what havoc has been created by the German raiders and how those remaining on the islands are re-acting to the attacks. This visit of Mr Beechman to the danger zone of the Scillies is characteristic of the interest that he takes in all parts of his constituency.

On Thursday, 5 September, the *Cornishman* stated that there was good news for evacuees as cheaper rail travel for parents was offered. It stated that on 8 September, cheap rail facilities for visiting evacuated children would be restored and the railway companies would introduce a number of new features designed to meet present working conditions. On the Great Western Railway, the traffic was so heavy that it was impracticable for the company to provide for visits by the ordinary week-day services, except on Tuesdays, Wednesdays and Thursdays. The company were, however, running certain special trains at weekends to the more distant reception areas. The Minister of Home Security stated that those who took advantage of the facilities to visit children in areas, to which pleasure travel was prohibited, would not be turned back. Each parent would be entitled, on application, to one monthly voucher, which would entitle the holder to a railway ticket at the specially reduced fare. Local authorities outside the London area had been invited to participate in the scheme.

On 7 September, the blitz of London began. It lasted for fifty-seven consecutive nights.

On 15 September, the RAF claimed victory over the Luftwaffe during the Battle of Britain.

On 17 September, child evacuees heading for Canada were killed while on board the SS *City of Benares* which was torpedoed and sunk by a German submarine.

The *Cornishman* of Thursday, 19 September, wrote about the recent raids on the Isles of Scilly. It stated that one of the most gratifying features of the circumstances emerging from the recent air raids on the Isles of Scilly was that, in spite of the fact that over 300 people left for the mainland, not one of them was in financial difficulties in their new homes, nor had anyone become a charge on the rates. Mainland authorities were amazed at the way in which the situation had worked out. They were, in fact, asking what had become of the Scillonian refugees to whose aid they were expecting to be called. What had happened appeared to be that for the most part the Scillonians had found homes with relatives and friends all over Cornwall. Others had had the good fortune to find employment almost immediately.

On 23 September, King George VI announced the creation of the George Cross.

Five high explosive bombs were dropped on RAF St Eval at 11.00 pm on 30 September. Although two landed on the aerodrome, little damage was done.

On 3 October, RAF St Eval came under attack again from German planes. Two Spitfires and one Avro Anson were completely destroyed.

The *Cornishman* of Thursday, 10 October, reported on an amazing discovery in a Cornish town. A bomb was found in a farmer's field six days after being dropped. The discovery was made by Mr T. Dawe, the tenant of the field. On the previous Wednesday morning, a bomb was dropped on the Cornish town and did tremendous material damage without causing loss of life. After the raid, deep ruts were found in a field at the top of the town and the theory put forth by the authorities was that these were caused by the bomb that had fallen and which had then ricocheted and eventually fallen on a garage at the foot of a hill a considerable distance away. Hundreds of people had since visited the spot totally unaware that any danger existed and residents slept in their beds feeling that they were perfectly safe instead of being possibly in

Children hide in a trench to shelter from enemy bombers. Britain became more of a target once Germany invaded France in 1940.

imminent danger. A member of the *Cornishman* visited the spot, by permission of the tenant. Mr Dawe informed him that he was about to fill in the rut. Hardly had he left the field, when Mr Dawe informed him that when he was scraping back the surrounding earth, his shovel struck something which gave out a metallic sound. Digging a little deeper, he disclosed the end of a cylinder. He immediately informed the authorities, who, on further excavations, found a bomb which they stated to be five cwt. This disclosure had caused the greatest alarm in the vicinity and showed how necessary it was that the public should be rigorously kept away from any area where a bomb had fallen. The bomb might have exploded at any minute, night or day, during the six days which had elapsed since it fell. The bomb was successfully removed on the following Wednesday morning by a bomb disposal squad and exploded.

On 14 October, RAF St Eval had its last attack when six high explosive bombs and twenty incendiaries were dropped on the base.

On 15 October, a unit of the Royal Indian Service Corps set up base at Duporth Camp, near St Austell. Their mules were stabled nearby at the old Savoy Cinema building in Truro Road.

The *Cornishman* of Wednesday, 23 October, carried a story about a battle off Land's End. It stated that a battle between British and German naval forces had taken place off Land's End on the previous Thursday. A joint Admiralty and Air Ministry communiqué issued on the Friday stated:

> Yesterday morning a force of German destroyers was sighted and reported by aircraft of the Coastal Command. The enemy flotilla, consisting of four ships, was steaming west of Brest. Visibility was low. British light forces in the vicinity proceeded at high speed to intercept and endeavour to bring the enemy to action. During the afternoon, the visibility cleared, and soon after 4 pm, one of our cruisers engaged the enemy at extreme range, in a position of about 100 miles southwest of Land's End. The enemy destroyers retired precipitately on being engaged. Our forces gave chase but the enemy, in the failing light, were able to escape into Brest. During their pursuit, enemy aircraft made two attacks on our ships but obtained no hits. Bombers of the Coastal

Command attacked the enemy. A bomb was seen to fall close to the bow of one enemy destroyer.

The news of the battle was served to the German people by Goebbels:

At the exit of the Bristol Channel, a naval battle took place between German destroyers and a British cruiser unit escorted by destroyers. Our destroyers attacked the enemy and scored a torpedo hit on a warship. The enemy thereupon broke off the engagement and German aircraft were sent to pursue them. The German destroyers returned to their base without having suffered damage.

The Admiralty and Air Ministry communiqué refuted the German claim by adding:

Today's German High Command communiqué not only states that an action between German destroyers and the British cruiser and destroyers took place at the entrance to the Bristol Channel, but claims that the German forces scored a torpedo hit on one of our warships. No damage was, in fact, sustained by any of our ships.

The Battle of Britain ended on 31 October.

The *Cornishman* of Thursday, 14 November carried a story about an air attack on the Isles of Scilly. It stated that the Air Ministry had announced on the previous night that the Islands of Scilly had been machine-gunned by a German plane, which caused no damage and casualties on the previous Sunday. The visit of the raider naturally caused much excitement. The attack lasted only a very brief period, it took place in the morning, and it was stated that the rear gunner of the plane opened fire as it flew across the islands. The plane appeared from the southeast, flying fairly high. Then it came down and opened fire. As it swept round and made a turn, its fire was returned from the ground, but the machine passed across the islands, firing one or two bursts as it went. Civilians stayed indoors and no one was hit.

Between 14 and 15 November, Coventry was heavily bombed by the Luftwaffe destroying the centre of the city. On 19 November, heavy bombing raids took place on Birmingham, West Bromwich, Dudley and Tipton. Southampton was heavily bombed on 23 November and

Bristol was hit the following night. The heavy raids on Bristol resulted in many people being evacuated.

The *Cornishman* of Thursday, 28 November, reported on a fight off the Lizard and the downing of an enemy plane. The story told how the inhabitants of Lizard village and the surrounding neighbourhood had had a thrilling sight on the previous Sunday, soon after midday, when they witnessed a fight between two Spitfires and a German bomber. The fight ended with the bomber, a Dornier, crashing into the sea just a little more than a mile from the Lizard headland. Two of its crew were rescued by the Lizard lifeboat. One was dead and the other was badly wounded. He had bullet holes in the face and one in the elbow. The rattle of machine-gun fire was the first intimation that the villagers had had of the approach of an enemy plane, which was then seen approaching at a great speed. Close on its heels were two British fighters. The excited villagers ran into the open to witness what was happening. The enemy bomber was flying so low that its markings could be plainly seen and it was losing height as it travelled. Not far from the village, the Spitfires circled round it and sent bullets crashing into it. The Dornier cleared the Lizard head by only a few feet as it headed out to sea, followed remorselessly by the Spitfires, which continued their relentless attack, and the German crashed into the sea about 2,000 yards distant. Those on shore hailed the sight with shouts of jubilation. Those who witnessed the sight included a large number of evacuee children from London.

Almost immediately after the enemy plane was seen to fall into the sea, Coxswain E. Stephens summoned his crew and the Lizard lifeboat was launched in an effort to save any survivors. He found two members of the bomber's crew.

Dr T.B. Newman was among the crowd who awaited the lifeboat's return and dressed the surviving man's wounds before he was taken to hospital. The injured man proved to be an air mechanic, who could not speak English, but in reply to an RAF officer, who spoke to him in German, he said he had been in the German air force for eight weeks only. Before this, he had served four years in the German army. The dead man, who was 21 years of age, was the wireless operator, and wore an Iron Cross, dated 1939. The lifeboat was again launched and searched the oil-covered sea for two hours, but could find no trace of the other two members of the crew. Before being removed to hospital, the injured German was taken to the Wavecrest tearooms where Mrs J. Charles gave him hot coffee and he thanked her in his own language.

During December, No 404 (later 1404) Meteorological Flight was formed at RAF St Eval. The operation was vital and provided essential weather data for missions.

The *Western Morning News* of Friday, 6 December, reported that a Dornier had been shot down off the Cornwall coast. It stated that the Dornier 17 was shot down just after 3 o'clock, the previous day, off the Gull Rock. A Hurricane pilot, flying low in cloud, saw a DO 17. He gave it one three-second burst of fire and saw the Dornier crash into the sea 2 miles from the coast. Mr J.P. Elliott, of Trephennel Farm, Portloe, interviewed by a *Western Morning News* reporter stated:

> Just after three o'clock, I was in a field above Portloe when I heard what seemed to me to be machine-gunning. I could not see anything but, immediately after, I saw a plane crashing down about 2 and a half miles out from Portloe and I saw what I thought to be a member of the crew who had baled out. The plane struck the water with great force. It went under at once and disappeared. About a minute later, the man came down near the same spot. Then I saw our Hurricane come racing back. Our plane had caught the Dornier just off Portloe, I should think.

Mr Fred Trudgen, of Portloe Post Office, said that he did not see it himself but one eyewitness, Gordon Trudgen, of Portholland saw the crash and saw one of the occupants of the German plane bale out. 'One of the Portloe boats went out with Tom and Gilbert Trudgen, Cyril Johns and a visitor towards the spot where the plane was thought to have gone down,' he said: 'But I believe that they went rather in the wrong direction and there was also some motor trouble. At any rate they did not find any survivors or anything. The sea was rather rough.'

Mr F.G. Connor said he did not see the plane crash, as he was in Portloe village, but his gardener, Gordon Trudgen, did so. When in the garden, the latter just caught sight of the plane flying and the next thing he saw was the crash into the sea. 'No one seems to have seen the fight between the Hurricane and the Dornier,' he added. Five South-West coastal towns and an inland town had had raids on the previous day without incident.

The *Cornishman* of Thursday, 12 December, stated that aliens must have permits if living within the county. It stated that when five Belgians had appeared at Penzance Police Court on the previous Monday, on a charge of failing to notify their departure to the Metropolitan Police, the Chief Constable of Penzance, Mr R. Jenkins, repeated a previous warning to aliens. Before leaving London, aliens must notify their intended departure to the police. The latter would notify him (Mr Jenkins) and it was in his power to stop aliens from coming into the district, which was a protected area. He had the power to order their departure and had done this in several cases. Many applications to come to Penzance and district came every week but it was his intention only to permit fishermen to enter in future. In view of the good record of the man in this case, he had proceeded only under the Aliens Order of 1920, which permitted him to let them remain, rather than under the more stringent Defence Regulations.

The Reverend B.J.S. Watkins receiving gifts at a toy service at Kenwyn Church in Truro. The gifts were to be delivered to poorer children living in the parish.

Between 12 and 15 December, Sheffield came under attack by the Luftwaffe and 660 people were killed. Liverpool was heavily bombed between 20 and 21 December with Manchester being blitzed the following night.

Supplies of goods in shops were short. However, trading up until Christmas was good as people bought what they could. Leave for the home forces was cancelled over the festive period. Christmas proved to be bomb free with no reported enemy attacks.

London was heavily bombed on the night of 29 December.

CHAPTER THREE

1941 – The Blitz

A government order came into effect in January compelling all businesses to inform fire-fighting services of the arrangements they had made for fire-watching. Fire-watching was made compulsory and all able-bodied citizens between 16 and 60 years of age were invited to assist in the work.

On 25 January, seven Heinkel bombers attacked St Eval dropping high explosive and incendiary bombs. Some missed their target falling in fields nearby. One bomb exploded near to the entrance of an air-raid shelter resulting in the deaths of twenty-two people.

ndon evacuees with a pair of newly-born nbs at Pullington Farm, Sweetshouse, dmin.

The *Western Morning News* of Monday, 27 January, carried the story of a raid on Cornwall. It reported that Union flags flew defiantly on the previous day over houses damaged when an enemy plane dropped two large bombs on a Cornish town during the Saturday evening. Five people were injured. People bombed out of their homes were machine-gunned by the raider as they raced for shelter, while a woman bravely went on digging out a man who was buried under the debris until urged by the latter to take cover from the shower of bullets. Many people had miraculous escapes. Mr Hawke and his mother-in-law, Mrs Alder, who suffered from multiple small cuts and shock, were the only hospital cases. Windows in houses and shops were broken.

Mrs G. Dunn and her three evacuee children had a miraculous escape. Their house was almost on the edge of the crater. When the explosion took place it collapsed, leaving only the walls standing. They were all indoors at the time yet escaped injury. The home of Mr and Mrs Hawke was badly damaged, the roof being stripped, windows and doors blown in and ceilings forced down. Mrs Hawke said that they were all in the front sitting-room. She had heard the plane very low and 'thought it was one of ours.' The next thing they knew was that they were all thrown towards the fireplace. There was a big explosion and things began to tumble all around them. 'I pushed my mother towards the staircase, and Mr O'Shea, a friend, dragged my husband outside,' she told the *Western Morning News*. 'While we were out there, the plane returned and started machine-gunning. We took cover behind the trees. It came back and opened fire a second time and we had to take cover again.'

One farm had a narrow escape. The bomb made a big crater in the field close to the farmhouse. The farmer stated, 'As the stones thrown out from the crater came crashing down on the roof of the farmhouse they sounded like bombs. One heavy boulder was hurled into the next field.'

On 5 February, the Air Training Corps was formed to provide

A view of Lemon Street in Truro covered in snow during the cold spell of January 1941.

The wedding of Lance-Corporal William H. Robins and Peggy Tabb at St Paul's, Truro during January.

An archway of bayonets was formed by members of the Truro Home Guard after the wedding of Harold Hay and Ivy Probis during February. The bridegroom's father and two brothers were all members of the Home Guard.

teenagers and young men with flying experience. Many would later join the RAF.

The *Cornishman* of Thursday, 6 February, carried a report about complaints from customers about the overcharging in hotels for rationed food. It reported that complaints had been made that, although rationing had reduced the size of meals in hotels, reductions had not generally been made in the charges. 'From all parts of Great Britain,' said the *Daily Mail*, 'hotel proprietors have written replying to these complaints.' In its issue for 30 January, it printed the following letter from Mr Robert Thomas (a hotel proprietor and mayor of Penzance):

Meat is certainly rationed, but take nearly all the other commodities required in hotels, which have

Cadets of the Camborne-Redruth squadron take instruction in Morse code. Here, they are receiving a message from an NCO.

A Polish refugee with two newly-born lambs at Home Farm, Tehidy. When she arrived in England, she could speak no English but within a short while, she was top of her class at school.

Mr F.W. Weatherhill explaining the structure of a plane wing to cadets of the Camborne-Redruth Air Training Corps at Dolcoath Technical School.

The Lord Lieutenant E.H.W. Bolitho taking the salute during the War Weapons Week parade in March.

increased in price from 50 to 100 per cent. As examples: fish, eggs, tinned goods (when you can get them), laundry, replacements of linen, even soap and toilet requisites and coal. True, the number, of course, is less, but has to be made up in a double portion of fish, poultry, game or whatever is going and the manager is at his wits' ends to know what he can do to vary the menu. My monthly tradesmen's bills are 17 and a half per cent more than they were before the war, with the same number of visitors.

The *Cornishman* of Thursday, 27 February, told that Flight-Lieutenant Arthur Forbes Johnson had been awarded the Distinguished Flying Cross and that he was born in Penzance in 1913. His present home was at Saltash, where his wife received the good news on the previous Thursday.

RAF Portreath was built during 1940 and opened in March 1941. It was initially a fighter command centre but became a stopping-off point for aircraft travelling onwards to the Middle East and North Africa. It later became a coastal command centre.

The *Cornishman* of Thursday, 6 March, told the story of a sole survivor who saw his shipmates die one by one off the Cornish coast. It reported that Richard Ayres, who was lying in Helston Cottage Hospital, Cornwall, after being dragged half dead from the sea, was the only survivor of a boatload of torpedoed British seamen.

Fire fighters taking part in the parade at the opening of the Camborne-Redruth War Weapons Week, the first effort of its kind in the county.

When his ship went down, he got away in one of the boats with twenty-nine shipmates. But after four days of intense cold and exposure, he saw his shipmates begin to die one by one until, at the end of several days, only two remained. The dead were buried at sea after a short prayer was said for each. Eventually, they made it to the Cornish coast, Mr Ayres, having navigated by the stars at night. They made flares with their clothes and although they attracted the notice of lifeboat-men, disaster followed. The boat was shattered by the rocks and Mr Ayres's two companions were too weak to reach the beach. Mr Ayres was hauled out of the water by Coastguard F.E. Gefford and Mr Peter Mitchell, half dead from exposure and shock. The other two were dead when they got ashore.

During the war, over 400,000 PoWs were held in camps within Britain. There were five major camps in Cornwall including White Cross Camp near St Columb Major, Scarnecross Camp in Launceston, Pennygillam Farm Camp, Consols Mine Camp in Tywardreath, Par and Bowithick camp on Bodmin Moor. However, there were many other camps that were not recorded. Many of the German and Italian

A small boy collecting daffodils at the beginning of spring at St Ives.

prisoners helped on the land and built roads and took part in the repairing of bomb damaged homes. They became friendly with the people they worked for and some married local girls after the war.

There was also a camp at Bake, Trerulefoot in Saltash (now the site of Bonds Timber Sawmill). This camp was small but housed a large number of Germans. Living quarters consisted of wooden bunk beds inside a row of Nissan huts.

The *Cornishman* of Thursday, 17 April, told of German airmen captured in Cornwall. Four Germans, the survivors of a Heinkel 111 which was shot down off the coast of Cornwall, on the previous Sunday afternoon, were captured by the Home Guard when they landed from a rubber boat at Pentargon, Boscastle. There were two officers and two NCOs who were handed over first to the Camelford police and then to

The remains of Mount Edgcumbe house after it was bombed in April 1941. It remained in this condition for many years before being restored in the 1950s.

The Earl of Mount Edgcumbe standing amongst the ruins of the house.

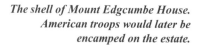

An aerial view of the badly damaged Mount Edgcumbe House.

The shell of Mount Edgcumbe House. American troops would later be encamped on the estate.

the military authorities. The captives, who were said to be surly, could not speak English.

On 21 April, 400 incendiary bombs, 30 high explosives and 2 paramines were dropped on Cornwall hitting Saltash, Cargreen, Torpoint and the Mount Edgcumbe areas.

The Italian Tower House at Cremyll was destroyed by German bombing during April 1941. Mount Edgcumbe House was gutted by German bombs on Tuesday, 22 April. Unfortunately, because of the bombing, many of the Edgcumbe family's possessions were destroyed. These included rare furniture and paintings. Three generations of the Edgcumbe family were painted by Joshua Reynolds and all but one painting were destroyed.

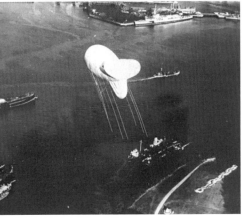

A barrage balloon flying at Thanckes, Torpoint during 1941.

It was said that both Adolf Hitler and Herman Goering coveted Mount Edgcumbe House as their country retreat were they to win the war so neither would have been best pleased when it was bombed.

On the 23 April, firemen from the ARP reported that they had put a fire out in the roof of the nearby Mashfords boatyard but had to let the tower burn due to the lack of water. During the bombing of Cremyll, three people lost their lives including the ferry skipper and an engineer.

On the same day, the naval stores at Thanckes, Torpoint were hit. The fires caused by the bombs burned for several days.

On Thursday, 24 April, the *Cornishman* reported that there had been crowded audiences at film shows put on for children at Penzance. The story told how three crowded, excited audiences filled the Centenary Hall in Chapel Street, Penzance, on the previous Monday, two in the morning and one in the afternoon. The shows were put on during exhibitions given for

A fire at the naval stores at Thanckes, Torpoint. The stores were hit by bombs on 23 April 1941. The fire burned for several days.

Children's Day in the Penzance and District War Weapons Week. The children, both locals and evacuees, greatly enjoyed the films, which were mainly supplied by the War Savings Movement and the Ministry of Information. There was one local picture, *The Saving of Bill Blewett*, in which the scenes of Mousehole greatly interested the children.

During the 6 and 7 May, 120 high explosives were dropped on Cornwall with incidents at Roskestal, Land's End to Bude and Penlee Point at Rame. Six people suffered slight injuries in the raids which damaged houses and buildings, including two at Torpoint. Minor damage was caused to buildings at Castle Park, Tor Farm and Trehan. A further 200 incendiaries and six high explosive bombs fell at St Germans and Minard but caused little damage. Saltash was hit by sixteen bombs.

The *Cornishman* of Thursday, 15 May, mentioned that more evacuees from Plymouth had arrived in Cornwall. It reported that

Bomb damage at Saltash which occurred during an attack on the night of 28 April 1941. A Mr and Mrs Allan died in the attack as did a Mr Olver who lived across the way.

another contingent of evacuees from Plymouth's blitzed area had arrived in Penzance early on Wednesday afternoon. They were 367 boys from Devonport High School and, in buses, they were taken to places to await their allotment to billets. After their arrival at Penzance, the lads were welcomed by the mayor (Alderman Robert Thomas) on the grounds of the Penzance County School for boys. The mayor expressed the hope that they would be happy in their new surroundings and said that the people of the borough would do all they

The remains of houses at Saltash after an aerial attack. The picture shows the back of houses in Higher Fore Street which were burned out after an enemy strike.

could to make their stay pleasant. The boys were taken to the Rookery, Marazion, the Institution at Madron, the Pavilion Theatre, Penzance, the Regent, Polytechnic, Queen's Western and Union hotels, Penzance, as well as to private houses.

In May, RAF Predannack opened as a satellite for RAF Portreath. It housed 247 Squadron complete with several Hawker Hurricanes whose mission it was to secure the night defence of the nearby ports and towns.

In the third week of May, the *Cornishman* reported that Penzance had had its first gas attack on the previous Saturday morning. The town had become strangely gas-mask conscious. Small boys and girls and mothers with their daughters out on morning shopping expeditions, all carried them and at the sound of the rattle, out of their natty carriers came the masks which were donned with the alacrity and precision of servicemen. The demonstration took place in the Market Place and Causewayhead, and residents heeded the warnings that had been given to them and came prepared to meet the consequences. The gas, tear gas, was released in the streets and clouds of it arose around the people. So well were masks adjusted that no one seemed to have suffered any ill-effects, although they found later that remains of the gas still lingered in the air and affected the eyes. An interesting feature was the way that the children responded. They all behaved calmly. Two schools, St Erbyn's and St Clare, brought their pupils along to undergo the test. Assistants at one company shop donned their gas masks during the attack.

On Thursday, 5 June, the *Cornishman* reported that Hayle Parish Council were seeking a compulsory fire-watching order. Mr J.H. Woolcock, at a meeting of Hayle Parish Council on the previous Saturday stated 'There are plenty of young men in Hayle who are not doing a thing, and who stop in bed and let others do the work, night after night.'

He moved a resolution to ask the West Penwith KDC to apply for compulsory powers to enforce the provisions of the Fire-Watching Order in Hayle. Mr R.J. Hammill (the Fire Prevention Officer) said he had in fact received a visit from the police only the day before and he hoped that meant that the police would assist to see that people were fulfilling their fire-watching duties, whilst they were out on their

A poster urging people to dig for victory and grow more food. Many planted potatoes and other vegetables in their gardens and allotments while public land, such as parks, was also used.

beats. No town, said Mr Hammill, had responded properly to the voluntary system of fire-watching and even at Penzance they had to get compulsory powers. The same thing would have to be done at Hayle. Mr Hammill said that the attitude of those who stayed in bed and did nothing was annoying and it seemed that they felt no alarm, nor was any appeal to them of any use. They appeared to think that the police and the ARP should deal with fire-watching. Mr Woolcock said someone was poisoning the minds of the people in Hayle and they were reluctant to fill in necessary forms, the suggestion being that, if they did, they would have to fire-watch anywhere in the West Penwith area. Such was not the case and Hayle people could rest assured that they would only have to watch fires in their own area.

Clothing was rationed from June 1941 and people were issued with booklets containing clothing coupons. People were told to 'make do and mend' so that clothing factories and their workers could instead produce munitions.

On Thursday, 24 July, the *Cornishman* told of four German airmen saved from an enemy bomber. The newspaper stated that a slim, slight figure, almost boyish in appearance, was to be seen in the police station at a southwest town on the previous Saturday morning. Wearing the steely blue uniform of the German air force with red swastika facings and high black boots, the youngster, 'with his pure Aryan appearance

A food coupons ration booklet which was presented to a shopkeeper every time food items were purchased.

Wartime jam-makers at Truro. Shown are members of the Truro Fruit Preservation Committee sterilizing jam jars at the fruit preservation centre in the city. The helpers had made several pounds of gooseberry jam but required more fruit.

and not unpleasant look,' seemed a trifle apprehensive of what was going to happen to him, but walked with head erect and his clean-cut features set hard. Despite his apparent youth, he held the Iron Cross and bar and was the pilot and commander of the aircraft. He was one of the crew of a Heinkel Bomber shot down off the south-west coast on the previous Friday afternoon and was landed with three of his compatriots at a south-west town early on the Saturday morning. The fifth member of the crew, the rear gunner, was presumed dead.

When their plane was shot down, some considerable distance from land, they were able to take to their rubber dinghy, from which, after several hours, they were picked up by a rescuing boat. From the latter, they were transferred to another craft, which brought them to the quayside. They were separated immediately after they had been picked up and placed below decks, one in each corner of the cabin, not a word was spoken, either by them or by their rescuers. Their arrival on land had been kept a closely-guarded secret, and, as they motored down to be handed over to the authorities, no one who happened to be about realized that four members of the Luftwaffe were so close at hand. This was the first occasion on which this particular town had witnessed the arrival of any Germans. At the police station, they were placed in separate cells and the local police guarding them had the (for them) somewhat unusual experience of being armed with revolvers. After they had been in the station for some time, they were interviewed individually and at length. Two of the men were taken by ambulance to the hospital of another south-west town, the others leaving on the Saturday evening by train for an unspecified destination.

On 15 August, the Southern Command issued a special order to all area commanders asking them to co-operate to the fullest extent with helping farmers to get in their harvest. Local commanding officers were asked to keep in touch with farmers in their vicinity so that, if necessary, they could help with the direct loan of personnel or make arrangements for requests to be met from other units. The army commander stated that assistance to farmers during the harvest was to be considered an urgent service. He added, 'The important point to remember is that the harvest must be collected quickly and safely.'

The *Cornishman* of Thursday, 28 August, reported on a Newlyn pilot's gallantry during an attack on a convoy. It stated that a daring operational flight by Pilot Officer William Thomas de Rouffignac Waters, RAFVR, of No 53 Squadron, of Newlyn, had won him the DFC.

In August, he had piloted one of two aircrafts which had attacked a convoy of one large merchantmen, escorted by five destroyers in the Borkum area. While taking avoiding action, a wing of Pilot-Officer Water's aircraft struck the water and the tip was torn off. Finding that his aircraft was flying correctly, he again attacked in a position which necessitated flying down the line of the enemy fire. Pilot-Officer Tom Water received the congratulations of a large circle of friends in the Penzance area, where he was well-known and was extremely popular. Before the war he had been in business with his father at Newlyn and for some seasons turned out for Newlyn Rugby Club.

At the beginning of September, it was reported that the jam ration was to stay. The increase in the jam ration to one pound a month was to remain until further notice, and not made for the month of August only, the Ministry of Food emphasized.

The *Cornishman* of Thursday, 4 September, reported on the coal shortage in the county. It stated that the Emergency Committee had reported to a meeting of the Cornwall County Council on the previous Tuesday that their attention had been drawn to the depletion of stocks of coal in the county and the inability of public utility undertakings to obtain fresh supplies. They had asked the ARP Controller to discuss the matter with the Deputy Commissioner. The Chairman (Colonel E.H.W. Bolitho) said the position was that they were quite as well off as many counties and better off than many areas. They knew the amount of coal in the county and, they stated, 'it was not the small coal scuttle that some people imagined.'

At the beginning of October, the *Western Morning News* reported on jam making in Cornwall. It said that voluntary helpers at Rilla

Many fruit preserving centres were set up in the county and members of Women's Institutes together with the WVS and other bodies made jam from home-grown fruit. The photo shows housewives dropping off their produce at one of the centres.

Mill Women's Institute, which was one of the two fruit preservation centres in Liskeard rural district, had made 4,036lb of jam. One ton had been sold and a second ton was for disposal. Describing this as a 'wonderful achievement,' the vicar of Linkinhorne (Reverend C. White) told Liskeard Rural District Food Control Committee on the previous Saturday that between twenty-five and thirty women had turned up each week, carried water a long way up a steep hill, and used equipment lent by parishioners. He mentioned that St Austell, which had been publicized for doing wonderful work, had only made half a ton of jam at their centre. The committee passed a vote of thanks to the workers at Rilla Mill.

A comment was made on the refusal of the Ministry of Food to supply householders with extra sugar for making their own jam, the Chairman (Mr A.T. Cock) pointed out that just as the blackberry season was over and hundreds of pounds had been wasted because of the lack of sugar to preserve the fruit, the Ministry had announced that extra sugar would be issued in November.

The *Western Morning News* of Monday, 6 October, reported

that supplies had been sent from Cornwall to Russia. It stated that Cornwall Central Hospital Supply Service had received a request for supplies for Russia and the same day had dispatched 400 pairs of bed socks, 200 helpless case shirts, 50 pairs of pyjamas and 50 operation stockings. It mentioned that five million wage-earners now made weekly contributions to the Red Cross Penny-a-Week Fund.

The *Western Morning News* of Friday, 7 November, reported on the government's criticism of salvage in Cornwall. It mentioned that there were thirty local authorities in Cornwall but during September, only twenty-five salvage returns had been received and of these, seven were nil.

The 25 had salvaged 155 tons of paper, 39 tons of metals, 59 tons of kitchen waste, 8 tons of bones and 6 tons of textiles. The total yield was £1,100, as compared with £641 in the September of the previous year. It was reported that it was too soon to see any results from Lord Beaverbrook's appeal but there had been a marked increase in paper salvage and for some months, the total receipts had been fairly level, the figures being £1,102 for both August and July.

Mr A. Hey, of Falmouth, the Ministry of Supply's official for the county, told a representative of the *Western Morning News*:

These details give the impression that those authorities working on the scheme are maintaining a constant flow. We want to get those sending nil returns to do something. The Ministry had hoped, before winter set in, to have the warehouses full of reasonable stocks of salvage but, sorry to say, the stocks are not where they should be but are in people's houses. With regard to kitchen waste, it is disquieting that there should be only three local authorities out of 30 that have tackled this job.

Mr. Hey emphasized that from the beginning, salvage had been a serious matter but now was vital to the country's interests:

'Some of the raw supplies we want are here,' he proceeded, 'and it is the job of all salvage officers to get them out. As I go about the county, I hear too often that salvage is not being collected and I am bound to say that, after investigation, I find most complaints could be remedied if the local authorities had better organized systems of collection. The fault is not always on the householder but too often lies at the door of the local authority. We all know that labour is scarce but there is a large amount of voluntary effort that could be used in our rural districts if it were only properly organized. Some of the districts in the county are doing remarkably well; some are doing remarkably badly. Salvage officers who say it cannot be done must be made aware that it must done. There is waste paper in this county which should be in the country's mills. We must have all those old books which have been on the shelves and which will never be read again. I cannot give the figures of the 30 districts in my area but I can say the average income from my own town is about £100 a month and it has been averaging that for many months. We have collected, on an average, about one ton of paper a month per thousand of the population. If those who read this will compare the figure with those of their own towns they will see where they stand. In view of the recent appeal by Lord Beaverbrook, I trust that all salvage officers in Cornwall will get down to the work and let us have the supplies.'

The *Western Morning News* of Friday, 14 November carried a story about children leaving Plymouth for Cornwall. It was reported that the children shouted and waved to their parents on the platform. There were three parties, numbering ninety-three in all, of Plymouth school children, between 5 and 13 years old, entrained at North Road Station on the previous day for destinations in Cornwall. Education officials, including Mr F.R. Glanville, Mr H.F. Curtis, Mr D.M. Symons and Mr R.L. Higham (the divisional evacuation officer), saw them off and the children were accompanied on the journey by teachers, women helpers and the Reverend A.D. Jago (the evacuation missioner, formerly curate of St Peter's, Plymouth). Children of St Mary's Roman Catholic School were specially catered for and were sent to another Roman Catholic school in a separate Cornish town.

On 25 November, the *Fisher Girl*, a requisitioned fishing vessel was bombed and sunk at Falmouth. On the same day, HMT *Jacques Morgand*, a British Royal Naval trawler was hit by the Luftwaffe and destroyed.

On 7 December, Japan attacked Pearl Harbor and declared war on America which had a direct effect on the people of Cornwall.

A Spitfire which had been donated by the people of Cornwall. It was named after the county.

Four days later, Germany and Italy also declared war on America. Americans were drafted into the services and were told that they could be sent anywhere in the world. President Roosevelt met with Winston Churchill in Washington and it was agreed that contingents of American troops would start arriving in the UK, mainly in the westcountry, in January 1942.

Red Cross vehicles at Truro. The mayor of Truro and Mr G.H. Johnstone welcomed the Red Cross display unit at High Cross, Truro, during December 1941.

The *Western Morning News* of Monday, 29 December reported on the year in Cornwall during 1941. It stated that in the past year practically everything in Cornwall had been overshadowed by the war effort and that when 'the terrific clash of arms' was over, it was likely to be found that one of the most satisfactorily accomplished tasks had been that relating to the harbouring of evacuees. As a county, it had not been regarded as a very vulnerable target for enemy action and to the Duchy were sent many thousands of children and adults from various parts of the country and bombed areas. The school population had been more than doubled in Cornwall. The influx of such huge numbers confronted local authorities with urgent and difficult problems but these were tackled with vigour and initiative and the authorities had been well backed by the population as a whole, who had been very willing and generous in providing accommodation for the homeless.

Officials from the big cities, from which the evacuees had come,

Members of the Women's Land Army topping sugar-beet at Treveor Farm near Truro during December.

in a raid__

Don't stand and stare at the sky. Take cover at once

A poster urging people to take cover immediately during an air raid. The picture shows a warden blowing his alert whistle.

A female worker completing the dirty work of servicing the tracks on a tank.

A trainee female worker using a power grinder.

On 17 November 1941, 30,000 tons of canned meat, fish and beans were distributed to shops. Most of the commodities came from the USA.

spoke highly of the reception and arrangements throughout the county and the headmaster of Devonport High School, which had been evacuated as a whole and accommodated in hostels in Penzance, had gone so far as to say that no authority in the country had tackled the problem so boldly or so successfully as the Penzance Welfare Committee.

The organization and consolidation of civil defence measures had occupied a good deal of attention. The County Council had made up a lot of leeway during the year and the ARP organization of the county was considered very good. The introduction of compulsory fire-watching proved to be a big job and in many places it had passed from voluntary to compulsion. The response was good. In some areas, the civil defence forces were tested under actual war conditions and had not been found wanting. Raids from enemy aircraft were numerous and a good many lives had been lost and considerable damage done to property. But the losses, regrettable as they had been, had been small considering the number and calibre of the bombs dropped, many of them having fallen harmlessly in open country. In all instances, the civil defence forces had done splendid work. Some assisted in the defence of Plymouth during the blitzes on the city.

All the industries of the county had naturally been affected by war conditions and, in regard to agriculture, things had been very difficult. Farmers, however, responded nobly to the appeal to increase the acreage under the plough and thus increase food production. During the year, 40,000 additional acres were treated and with 50,000 additional during the previous year and 25,000 more for 1942, there was about 243,000 more acres under the plough, than at the end of the last war. The small holder had been hit rather badly and Cornwall was a county of small holdings. Orders were issued to reduce stocks of pigs and poultry, the fear being a shortage of feeding-stuffs, but the shortage had not been as great as anticipated and pigs were increasing again. Requests were made to double the acreage for potatoes which, on the whole, were a very fair crop, and where the crop was poor the subsidy of £10 an acre had helped. Cattle and sheep had come to market in very fair condition. Wheat looked well for the next harvest, with hardly any failures, and the last harvest had been quite good, while crops of broccoli and cabbages had rarely looked better. Labour had been short but with tractors and the help of Land Army girls the work had been done. School children had helped, especially with the potato crop. Wages had been raised to £3 a week but farmers did not mind that the government implemented their promise to raise prices and did not delay over it.

The year 1941 had not been a good one for Cornish mining. The average price of tin was a little below that of the previous year and was certainly not high enough to cover the rising cost of other materials. Coal, for instance, was nearly double the price it was a short time previously and other materials had gone up similarly. The result had been that Cornish mining, while helping to pay for the increased wages of some of the other industries, had not been able to pay better wages itself and there had been a consequent shortage of labour. It was only to be expected that unskilled labour could earn better money elsewhere where it was not going underground. This shortage of labour

Fishermen taking in their catch. The fishing industry continued throughout the war and provided vitally needed food.

had been a serious problem in the industry during the last year. It had been impossible to get enough men to carry out what was required to be done and tin production had decreased on account of it. Owing to general conditions, Polberro had had to close down and the only mines working in the county were East Pool, which was actually threatening to close down, Geevor and South Crofty and even they were working on a reduced scale. There was plenty of metal in the county, if the money could be found to extract it.

Fishermen operating off the Cornish Coast had undoubtedly had a very good year during 1941. Already the effect of the absence of trawlers had been noted. Since they had not been present to break up the shoals, fish had been very much more plentiful and catches had been good. Prices had also improved and even the control figures had been better than those reached during the natural market conditions of peace time. With the exception of the shell fishery, all branches of the industry had been successful. The St Ives herring season had been disappointing but the winter fishing generally had been good. Deep sea lining had been stopped since the collapse of France. A few boats had carried on this fishery close in shore and these had done very well. The shell fishery had suffered from the fact that Admiralty regulations had prevented the men from getting to their grounds but the situation had been compensated by the fact that the prices realized for the fish that had been landed had been good. One point that had caused some concern, however, had been the heavy call up of the younger men. This had been rather serious, especially when the boats had been deprived of engineers. Fishing boats, generally, were not equipped with self-starting engines and men over 70 years of age, who now formed some of the crews, found it a great strain to swing them. An appeal had been made for the retention of the engineers, whoever else may be taken from the crews, but so far it had had no effect. Generally speaking, the outlook for the fishery was quite a bright one and recruits were coming to it who would not had dreamt of doing so some time ago.

The second year and the first three months of the third year of the war had seen the china clay industry reach almost its lowest level since its development made it the largest heavy industry in Cornwall. Very few overseas markets were now open, although there had been some shipments to America during the year and a certain amount of clay was still shipped to a few other countries. It was not possible to give even an approximate idea of the tonnage of clay produced and transported during the year but it was probable that the home market, which used to be one of the smallest, by comparison with the others, had become one of the largest now that the others were closed. One of the most important events of the year in the clay industry had been the scheme for concentrating production at a limited number of works. This had been largely designed to permit the drafting of thus created surplus labour into specifically war industries. Hundreds of men, many of them of more than military age, had gone to munitions and other factories and scores more had become security men at aircraft works 'up country'.

At Christmas, 1940, the clay workers received a further war bonus. This, however, was again under review, and a still further bonus could be awarded. There was an articulate demand for a wage no less than the £3 a week which the farm workers had been awarded.

Cornwall did very well during War Weapons Weeks in the earlier part of the year, when between £2,000,000 and £3,000,000 was raised, and by Warship Weeks up to date well over £1,000,000 had been raised.

Camborne headed the list in the former effort with £480,000 and up to the present for Warship Weeks (others had yet to be held) and Penzance led the way with £240,269. Truro raised £226,057, St Austell £219,710, Falmouth £130,000, Liskeard £100,666, Helston and Kerrier £86,000. Fowey £27,226 and St Ives £62,059. Each district exceeded its objective.

CHAPTER FOUR

1942 – Run Rabbit Run

The *Cornishman* of Thursday, 8 January reported on a mock invasion of Cornwall. The article stated that Cornwall had had a taste over the past weekend of what might be expected 'should Hitler try and implement his threats to attack these shores.'

A full-scale invasion exercise was undertaken by a large body of military and all the Civil Defence Services, the objects being to test out these Services and also to get the public invasion minded.

There were scores of realistic incidents and the exercises, besides proving valuable to the participants, found a splendid reaction on the part of the civilian population.

The weekend's activities were watched by General Sir Hugh Elles, Regional Commissioner for the South-West; Mr H. Medland, Deputy Regional Commissioner and high military officials. Sir Hugh afterwards paid tribute to the keenness with which members of the Civil Defence Services had operated. He said the whole history of the exercise would be closely studied and an inquest held on the results.

Large numbers of the county's Civil Defence Services co-operated with the military when a full-scale invasion exercise was held in Cornwall.

Military formed the enemy, most of whom were supposed to have been borne to the county by air, and there were a few landings by sea, while military, Home Guard and Civil Defence Services co-operated in the defences. It was estimated that, including firemen and police, about 5,000 ARP personnel took part. 'Casualties' were provided by

Girl Guides, Boy Scouts, fire-watchers and ATC members and there were plans to deal with 2,000 casualties in the 24 hours the exercise took place - from 5.30 pm on Saturday to 6 o'clock on Sunday evening.

Loud-speaker cars were sent round the towns and districts, intimating that gas would be used and advising people to stay in their homes, the result being that very few were out without their masks.

Tear gas was used in a number of places but few people were caught napping. In one town, the Sunday dinner was disturbed when people came to their doors to watch the enemy forces slipping cautiously down the sides of the streets.

The general idea was that sea and air attacks had taken place on Cornwall and the enemy was trying to capture towns to form a line across the peninsula, to cut if off and form a bridgehead from which to attack the rest of England. Some towns were captured. Defence committees in the localities sat throughout the night and in one town, twelve hostages were taken and the demand was made of the Defence Committee of all reserves of foodstuffs, 3,000 loaves, all hospital stores and 100 head of cattle. The latter were to be slaughtered and dressed by 9 o'clock in the morning and two 'hostages' were to be 'shot' every hour in which the demand was not met.

In another town, the 'enemy' took twenty hostages and wanted all the horses in the town and sufficient food by 7.30 am, or the hostages would be shot but the 'enemy' left the town before the demand could be exercised.

In another town which was captured, the Defence Committee retired to a second stronghold and were not discovered. They were still sitting there during the day and in touch with the ARP and surrounding villages, the enemy searching for them but unable to find their hiding place.

A supposed landing by parachute took place in a certain locality near an important town, which was subsequently captured and then the enemy moved towards an adjoining town but they were misdirected, took the wrong road and were led into an ambush. In another town, which was captured, some citizens actually gave information which led the enemy direct to the police headquarters.

In the northern part of the county, a town was taken at 3.30 am in the morning but there was a counter-attack later from a still more northerly direction.

In a southern part, there was an attack and the reaches of a river were gained without any opposition. There was an air landing in the direction of an important town, where the defenders had a difficult task because of the size of the landing force. The Home Guard men gave good account of themselves but the attackers occupied the outskirts of the town, although they did not take it.

One important borough fell during the afternoon when the railway station, Post Office and police station were seized, and where the Town Hall was supposed to have been destroyed by bombs and the Chairman of the Defence Committee killed.

A Quisling took control of one town and issued a threat to the Defence Committee, giving them a time limit in which to meet his demands. Home Guards raided the Quisling's headquarters while he was resting and shot him.

Some of the Fifth Columnists were disguised as women and in one district two War Reserve policemen became suspicious of one and followed her. They eventually arrested her, when she was revealed to be a soldier acting as a Fifth Columnist. Telephones were supposed to have been cut off from 10 o'clock in the morning and other means of communication had to be brought into operation for the remainder of the exercise.

High-explosive and other bombs were deemed to have been dropped in a good many places and important buildings set on fire. On the other hand, roads leading to key points were bombed to prevent reinforcements moving up, and one plan by the enemy to run troops into a town by putting an extra coach on a train was frustrated by the defender 'blowing up' the bridge.

General Elles stated after the exercises: 'One of the lessons of the exercise is that it has shown the utility of the public obeying a stay-put policy during emergency.'

Whilst people generally did as they were told, there were instances of defenders being hampered by sightseers, particularly children, but it was felt that it would not have been practicable to have kept the general public completely off the street in what, after all, was only a mock invasion but they would have adopted a very different attitude had there been a real invasion. The exercises showed, too, the prime necessity of people carrying gas masks and identity cards.

Whilst most people had these requirements, there were instances of persons being caught unawares when tear gas was released.

A notable instance of failure to have gas masks handy was furnished by the city fathers at one place. They were in session as a Defence Committee endeavoured to keep the life of the place going. But they had not got their gas masks with them and when a smoke bomb was flung into the place where they were sitting, they had to go through the gas to get to their masks in another part of the building. There was only one exit in their place of session. Some, it was found, had not got their masks at all. Another point, already referred to, was the need for absolute silence on the part of civilians in the matter of directing enemy forces. Of course, in the exercises, many did not know which side was which, a fact which would not arise in an actual invasion, when in any event, the request for information by any invader, who might have succeeded in effecting a landing, would scarcely be as polite as those made over the week-end. All things considered, however, it was felt that the Civil Defence Services and the general public co-operated well with the military. Many valuable lessons had been learnt, and whilst it was not claimed that everything was perfect or that there were not errors which would have to be rectified, the purpose of the weekend had, to a large extent, been achieved.

Mrs C.H. Beauchamp, head of the Cornwall Hospital Supply Service, helping to pack a hamper of articles at Truro, destined for Russia as part of the Aid for Russia appeal.

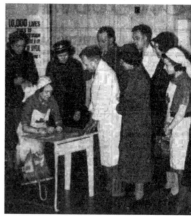

The Cornwall campaign appealing for 10,000 blood donors opened at Camborne during February. Many volunteers turned up including shop workers, housewives and nurses. The drive was part of Army Blood Transfusion Scheme.

The *Western Morning News* of Friday, 27 February noted that Cornwall was the next county in the Ministry of Works agenda to be

The smiling faces of evacuees in Cornwall. The mayor (Mr Harold Thomas) is pictured with the children, most of whom were from Plymouth, at the opening of an evacuees club in Truro where they met for games and recreation.

swept for scrap metal. Starting early in March, Ministry of Works teams would be setting up headquarters in Cornwall and would search each district systematically for all idle metal but particularly iron and steel. The provisional date for the start was 6 March.

Dumps of scrap metal were the first objectives. The Ministry of Works had the task of finding 40,000 tons of metal per week, in addition to metal recovered through normal trade channels. The USA needed all her scrap for her own factories, so the UK had to find its own. It was stated that the colossal task could be accomplished but only if everyone helped. No metal was to be left idle. Unwanted iron bedsteads, broken mangles or sewing machines, perambulator frames, fenders, fire-irons, keys that once fitted long forgotten locks, broken garden mowers, nuts and bolts and old spare parts from the garage. 'Every house in the county can find this sort of metal,' it was announced.

Ministry of Works officials would locate and schedule metal which may have to be demolished and idle metal lying about in builders' yards, workshops, smithies and garages.

They were anticipating the co-operation of Cornish local authorities and organizations, such as the WVS, Women's Institutes, ARP services, youth organizations and farmers.

The Ministry of Works guaranteed that every existing dump in Cornwall would be cleared during the drive but asked that each dump be increased to at least four times its present size.

During February, Douglas Vosper, a member of the Saltash Boy

Scouts' volunteer trailer pump crew, attached to the Saltash Fire Force received a BEM at Buckingham Palace. The crew was particularly active and useful during raids on the area. High explosive bombs killed a Scout and seriously injured two others. Mr Vosper drove the victims to a first aid post and then returned to fight the fires throughout the night and next day. His home was at Bostraze, Callington Road, Saltash.

Sir Stafford Cripps announced to the House of Commons in February that extravagance was a thing of the past and there should be no petrol used for pleasure driving. He also said there would be a cut in clothing rations and sporting events should be curtailed. Silk stockings were no longer available and many women coloured their legs with gravy browning to give the desired effect.

Group Scoutmaster Douglas C. Vosper of Saltash who helped put out fires in a goods yard whe other members of h troop were injured. He was awarded the British Empire Med at Buckingham Palace during February 1942.

The *Western Morning News* of Thursday, 26 March reported on soldiers' needs in Cornwall. It stated that Cornwall Joint Service Comforts Organization had met on the previous day at Truro to discuss the problems and special needs of Service men. The Lord-Lieutenant (Lieutenant-Colonel E.H.W. Bolitho) who presided, said Cornwall was still considerably behind other counties. It was difficult with the sum at their disposal to do anything like enough, not only for comforts, but for recreation and all the sides of welfare which should be catered for. They must take steps to get more money, aiming at least for £1,000. Mrs Maclaren, secretary and chairman, reported that the bulk of their gifts had gone direct to men in Cornwall and ships in South-West ports, but at special request, consignments had been sent to the Middle East, Iceland, Russia and the North Sea. In two years, they had issued 54,074 knitted garments and thousands of books. The work was growing and in the last six months, they had received 32 cwt. of knitted gifts. They had been at pains not to compete with other organizations.

Admiral Sir Henry Kitson expressed the gratitude of the navy for all the comforts which had been sent. Major Eaton Hart expressed thanks for the army and appealed for furnishings for quiet rooms for studious men. They wanted to set up about eight such rooms in the county. It was their duty to provide something better for the studious men than cinemas and dance halls. Lady Vivian said that she would be glad to appeal to the WVS to help in any way. Mrs Le Grice, president of Cornwall Women's Institutes, thought if an appeal was made to the Women's Institutes there would be a good response. Colonel G.T. Williams, the county welfare officer, said that men in isolated spots, scattered all over the county, had no amusements of any description. They were trying to help them before anybody else. Brigadier W.V. Buckley, the secretary of Cornwall Territorial Army Association, also stressed the need of quiet rooms for older soldiers.

The *Cornishman* of Thursday, 23 April carried the story of money raised by evacuees. It told that on the previous Friday evening, the members of the Pavilion Club, who were all evacuated from London, gave a repeat performance of the concert held the previous week.

So popular was the first concert that the success of the second was assured and it was little wonder that the members were able to hand over the amount of £14 14s 0d to the West Cornwall Hospital.

A crowded house again enjoyed the concert on which so much time and trouble had been spent by the London mothers and their children.

An American gift to Cornwall. Colonel E.H.W. Bolitho accepted two emergency food vans on behalf of Cornwall County Council during April 1942. The vans were the gift of Henry Ford and his son, Edsel. The photo shows members of the council and Civil Defence representatives after the ceremony.

Shortly before dusk on Tuesday, 28 April, a British fighter intercepted and destroyed a German bomber off the north coast of Cornwall.

The *Western Morning News* of Friday, 1 May carried a story about what Cornwall would do if it was invaded. At a special meeting at Truro on the previous day, the Cornwall Federation of Chambers of Commerce and Traders' Association mentioned the important subject of maintenance of food and other essential supplies in the event of invasion. The military commander of the county discussed the preparations necessary to maintain these supplies in the case of an enemy attack. The President, Mr E. Trounson, said that at their last meeting they inquired whether they were prepared, from a business point of view, for invasion, and they all answered 'No.' But now they had moved ahead very rapidly and those working on it for some time were delighted at the steps taken. The commander spoke of the splendid spirit of desire to co-operate with those in charge of the military situation. He reviewed the military situation and pointed out the steps that would be taken in regard to the Home Guard and other forces.

If air landings took place, they were prepared for any possible confusion. Everybody would have to carry on as best as they could until things were sorted out.

They looked to the Home Guard for accurate information and delaying action and it was expected that, after forty-eight hours, the situation would begin to clear up. If Cornwall were not invaded, it was the intention that normal life should go on as far as possible.

Food was very important in keeping up morale and carrying on life in general, and food would be controlled from the county headquarters. There had been a good deal of worry about the distribution of food but that had been gone into very carefully and, he added, 'I don't think we ought to starve.'

Answering questions, the commander said that the scorched earth policy was not one adopted in this country, the reason being they expected to turn the Boche out.

Asked about permission for members of the Home Guard to help in the corn harvest, when badly wanted at home, the commander said instructions were to give every consideration to farmers at their busiest periods in peacetime. The regular army was available to give help to farmers and if agricultural help were wanted from soldiers, he would do what he could if he were communicated with. The president remarked that every person would be entitled to a ration of biscuits,

A steam roller flattening out scrap metal at Penryn as part of the countrywide scrap metal collection campaign.

The king and queen with Belgian fishermen during their visit to Cornwall in May.

The king and queen walking between lines of Land Girls whom they inspected on a visit to a Land Army Hostel at Penzance.

The king and queen at Truro railway station during May 1942. Also pictured are the mayor (Mr H. Thomas) and the Lord-Lieutenant (Colonel E.H.W. Bolitho).

The mayor and mayoress of Falmouth (Mr and Mrs R.E. Gill) who welcomed the royal visitors on arrival at Falmouth station.

The king and queen leaving the shaft head of South Crofty, Camborne, where they saw some of the machinery in action.

bully beef, milk, margarine, sugar and tea. Supplies were already in the county and the public would be advised what they had to do if their villages were cut off. They wanted to keep people at home and the roads left for the military.

Asked by the Chairman (Mr Hartley Thomas) if he were happy as to the relationship between the Home Guard and the police, the commander said the police were part of the organization of defence, and their organization was extraordinarily good. If invasion took place, the military would be in charge and police would be under their jurisdiction. Acknowledging a vote of thanks, the commander said it was important in defence that all should work together. The president observed that in the event of invasion they would be completely under the orders of the commander and that the people, who ought to be in touch with each other, were now in touch. Unless anything very dire happened, everybody in Cornwall would be fed.

The *Cornishman* reported that fresh supplies of oranges would be available in the shops in Cornwall from Thursday, 28 May and would be reserved for a period of five days for issue at the rate of 2lbs per head to children in possession of a green ration book. After the five days reservation period had elapsed, surplus oranges were to be sold to other customers but retailers were asked to give priority to children, schools, hospitals and invalids.

The *Western Morning News* of Tuesday, 16 June carried a story about hospitality in Cornwall. It told that county hospitality was needed for tired and convalescent workers, for members of the civil defence, known as the Fourth Arm. The previous year, about 250 guests had come to Cornwall to find rest and renewed strength.

Miss Garrett, of Tower Park, Fowey, was hostess to more than 100 civil defence workers the previous year and Mrs Carter, of Manaccan, was second to her in providing hospitality.

During the past three months, hospitality had been arranged in Cornwall for London workers and eleven from Bath and Bristol.

'One hostess,' it was said, 'found that when her guest arrived from Bath, he had been recommended for the George Medal; he was the second George Medallist to be given rest and hospitality in Cornwall.'

Miss Smith told the *Western Morning News* that Mrs Woollcombe was working out a scheme which would enable them to go to any town to offer rest and hospitality to those civil defence workers who may have been badly knocked about.

Mrs Singer revealed that last year, there were sixty-four hostesses in Cornwall under the scheme and she hoped that there would still be as many as there were then. She also stated that the staff house at Benenden School, and part of the accommodation used at Bude by Clifton College, would probably be used this year as rest hostels for civil defence workers in all services of the Fourth Arm.

Miss Smith said that every civil defence worker needing rest was interviewed so that the right people were sent to the right places. A man could take his wife, or a wife her husband, if necessary; but no children were allowed.

The *Cornishman* of Thursday, 25 June reported on the use of women within the police force. At a special meeting of the Cornwall Standing Joint Committee on the previous Saturday, the chairman (Mr A. Browning Lyne) reported that he had told the chief constable to go ahead with providing alternative female police for the younger members of the force, who would in the near future be called up. The

HRH the Duke of Kent visiting Camborne during July 1942 where he met Civil Defence workers. Also pictured is Mrs P.R. Evans of the ARP control staff.

Home Office had agreed to a certain scheme to supplement these men but had it involved any substantial amount of money, he certainly would not have given the chief authority to go ahead. By arrangement with the Home Office, it would not involve the county in much more than £25 a year.

It was mentioned that there was difficulty finding suitable women to do the work. 'They would not, perhaps, do a police constable's work to the same extent as the male but it was thought women could replace these men and keep the force going reasonably well,' it was stated.

The chief constable (Major E. Hare) said he had already booked half the number required and expected no difficulty getting the remainder.

The *Western Morning News* of Friday, 10 July carried a story about the royal visit to Cornwall. It stated that HRH the Duke of Kent continuing his Cornish tour, had had another busy day. He had spent two hours at Geevor Mine, Pendeen and, in addition to other duties, carried out inspections of ARP and other personnel at St Just, Helston and Penzance.

At Geevor, he descended a tin mine for the first time in his experience. While underground, he used a drilling machine and on the surface was handed some tin oxide with a Cornish shovel.

This was a most instructive visit, for he witnessed the whole process of tin mining, from the winning of the ore in the depths of the mine to the dressing floors, where the final material was obtained for the market.

Geevor Mine, which had been working for many years and

continuously by the same company since 1911, was one of the three principal producing mines in the county, the others being East Pool and South Crofty. It was 1,300 feet in depth.

The duke only descended to the 600ft. level, the journey down occupying thirty seconds. He was attired in the usual rig-out of overalls, gum boots, miner's helmet and light and was accompanied by the Lord-Lieutenant (Lieutenant - Colonel E.H.W. Bolitho), who was his host during his stay in the Duchy; the manager of the mine (Mr W.E. Sevier), who explained the various workings and processes; and the underground manager, or mine captain, Mr W.C. Evans.

He descended the Victory shaft, so named because it was constructed during the last war, and on arrival at the level went through a long tunnel, lit by small lamps, to a spot where men were engaged in drilling. There was a deafening roar as the party approached, the drills being worked by Messrs John Andrewartha and John James, two old employees.

The machines were stopped and, after the royal visitor had asked questions of the manager, he spoke to the two men inquiring how long they had been employed there – one twenty-five years and the other twenty-eight years. He asked that the machines should be restarted and for some minutes worked one of them as the miners had been doing. He then retraced his steps along the tunnel and went to the wince, where he climbed up the face of the tunnel and along a very rough piece of ground, at the end of which miners were doing piece-work. The duke exhibited considerable agility in getting about the place. He was shown how the staff picked out the wince which came down chutes and into trams. On the way back to the cage, he came across several miners having their break. He inquired what they called it and one replied. 'A morsel' but that in the Camborne district it was called 'croust'.

Asked what they partook of, the reply was that it was sometimes pasties and sometimes cake.

The party were underground for about three parts of an hour.

On arrival at the surface, the duke was cheered by a number of women and children who had assembled at the pit head, and spoke to some of the women, including Mesdames Matthews, G. Eddy, H. Kemp, L. Edwards, W.T. Nicholls and J. White. They were all miners' wives and Mrs Matthews congratulated his Royal Highness on the birth of a son.

For this, he thanked her and then inquired if the women had plenty of food and if they kept gardens.

Passing to the various works on the mine, he inspected the washing plant, the ball mill, saw women engaged at the picking belts picking off waste granite and he also witnessed the crushing process in the concentration section, with vanning and James tables, the slimes plant and dressing floors. It was at the last point that he took a Cornish shovel and handled some of the material ready for the market.

In the course of the tour, he talked with Mr E. Trembath, a workman who mentioned that he served in the Collingwood in the last war with the king. He also spoke to G. Maddern, aged 17, who was engaged in buddling, who told the duke his wages were 5s 6d a day and that he had been on the mine for the two years since leaving school.

In the afternoon, there was a large parade at Helston, where His Royal Highness was received by the mayor (Mr L.W. Oliver), who was accompanied by members of the corporation and members of the civil defence who were introduced to the duke.

His Royal Highness took quite a long time going through the ranks, talking to many of those on parade and asking them questions as to their service, how many hours they devoted to it each week and if they liked the performance of their duties.

The parade of the personnel of the civil defence organizations for St Just and Pendeen, when they were inspected in the morning by the duke, was marshalled in the Square at St Just. Including a strong contingent of the WVS, there were about 300 on parade. Arranged around three sides of the ARP workers were the school children of the district, carrying banners, flags and innumerable bunches of flowers. Altogether, it was a very pretty sight which greeted his Royal Highness as he stepped from his motor-car and received a great welcome from the excited youngsters.

His Royal Highness had a word with many of those on parade. He spoke to Mr F.C. Attwood, who had served in the Canadian army in the last war, and with Mrs Jean Fraser, the only woman warden in the district, who was bombed out of her home in Kent, where she had been doing the same work.

Two boys of the Army Cadet Corps were very pleased when he inquired about their drills and school work. Every now and then, the duke left the parade and had a word with the expectant school children. It was a delightful gesture and much appreciated by the youngsters.

Nor were the members of the general public forgotten. His Royal Highness spoke to several, including one or two evacuees, and said he was pleased to hear that they were so well treated by their Cornish hosts.

Mrs R.J. Harvey, of St Just, who was present with her three children, all under school age, said the duke inquired about her husband, who was in the Middle East, and expressed his pleasure that she had recently received two letters from him. In conversation with Mr James Rowe, chairman of St Just Urban Council, the duke said it had been a wonderful parade and he was delighted with his reception.

The *Western Morning News* of Friday, 21 August carried a story about a proposed exercise in Cornwall. A largely attended meeting at Truro on the previous day considered a proposed military and civil invasion exercise over a portion of Cornwall and passed a resolution that it was expedient that such an exercise should be carried out and consented to orders being made for the closing of shops, licensed premises, all premises for the purposes of entertainment, to which the public were admitted, and for the restriction of traffic.

The Lord-Lieutenant, who presided, said the exercise would be on a larger scale than ever before attempted and the idea was to exercise the population in invasion-mindedness, similar to that carried out at Bristol, and which meant the closing of public houses, shops and cinemas during the period of the exercise. Those present representing agriculture, trade, entertainment and others were asked to co-operate. Brigadier Rawson, of the Regional Commissioner's Office, said the specific purposes were to educate the general public as to what they might be confronted with and what their duties should be in the event of an invasion; to ensure as many people as possible are capable of doing a job of work and being detailed to do some definite form of duty when invasion came; to organize them in such a way that they could carry out their duties satisfactorily; to practise with the armed forces and civil defences to co-operate so as to form a coherent whole and ensure one united front, and to stimulate generally the war mentality and effort.

The general public would have two main duties. One, to stand firm and the other to help the military and other authorities to beat the invaders. That could only be done by organization. He quoted what was done in Bristol which was a considerable success and a landmark in civil defence organization. He mentioned the military side of the exercise and in regard to the civil side, he said if they were to get the public to play cheerfully the problem must be put to them clearly and forcibly.

It must be put over by personal contact and it was best done by the personal influence and instruction of air-raid wardens, WVS and the Fire Guard service, who should keep in touch with every street and alley in the towns or rural districts.

Propaganda, he urged, should be cumulative, reaching its peak just before the exercise. Three weeks before, bulletins should be issued, dealing with general topics and civil defence, forces should make their contacts with people, telling them the way to take their part and should start registering people for jobs.

A fortnight before, a second bulletin should be issued, explaining the Invasion Committee organization, the object and the manner which the public could take part, and the wardens, WVS and Fire Guards would again take to their streets and organize them into parties.

A considerable number of the public would be asked to act as casualties or evacuees; some would be asked to help in the distribution of food, unloading and loading of foodstuffs, removing stocks from damaged and threatened buildings, to assist generally with emergency food arrangements, to help with water, in emergency cooking arrangements, treatment of casualties, reinforcing the medical side, clearing roads of debris, filling in bomb craters and filling sandbags etc.

A month before the exercise, the Emergency Committee should hold public meetings, with representatives of churches, licensed victuallers, tradesmen etc. No war production was to be interfered with. All bona-fide railway passengers would be allowed to obtain refreshments at railway stations and there would be no restriction on the opening of churches. Answering questions, it was stated that every form of entertainment would cease, but milk distribution would be allowed. No interference was wished for in regard to Sunday church services. Reverend J.H. Pritchard (the chairman of Cornwall Methodist District) said he would welcome definite instructions from higher authorities as to the line to be taken regarding church services, and Mr N.E. Purcell (vice chairman of the County Council) thought it would be better to relieve ministers of responsibility and issue an order that no Sunday morning services should be held. The chairman said he thought he

A hoarding showing the totals collected during War Week in 1942.

could safely say that no order would be given which would interfere with the holding of services during the exercise.

The *Western Morning News* of Friday, 21 August reported on a court case involving mispriced food. It told that at Falmouth Police Court on the previous day, Stanley Rowe, of Messrs W. Rowe and Co, fruiterers, of Market Street, Falmouth, was summoned for selling canned beans at 10d per tin, the official price being 7d, and Miss Irene Johnson, an assistant in the shop, was summoned for aiding and abetting him. Mr A.H. Thrall represented the local Food Control Committee and Mr R.L. Frank, the defendants. Mr Thrall stated a complaint was made to the Food Control Committee by a customer that he had been charged 10d for a 7d tin of beans. Mr H.E. Turner, the enforcement officer, visited the shop and asked Miss Johnson the price of a tin of beans. She replied 10d and produced a tin exactly the same size as that bought by the customer who made the complaint. He asked her how she arrived at the price and she pointed to a list on the wall.

Mr Turner reminded her that 10d was the price for runner beans and then Miss Johnson said she had made a mistake. The figures ten were close to the figure seven. The prosecution did not suggest there was anything sinister in the transaction but he had to point out that the increased charge amounted to 40 per cent. Mr Frank assured the court that it was a pure mistake. The assistant unfortunately misread the figures. When the gentleman who made the complaint heard the assistant's explanation, he was perfectly satisfied and received his overcharge back. He also tried to withdraw his complaint but it was too late. There was no attempt at black marketing or making illicit profit. Miss Johnson said she would not have charged 10d if she had known it was a mistake on her part. She told Mr Turner she had sold hundreds of tins of beans but she did not think she charged 10d for each one. Mr Turner stated the assistant told him the firm had sold thousands of tins of beans. There was no suggestion that Messrs Rowe had set out to make an illegal profit. The Chairman, Mr W. Chappel, said the Bench could not accept the explanation that a mistake had

A company inspection of Cornwall cadets by Colonel E.H.W. Bolitho, accompanied by Colonel C.F. Fleming and Lieutenant-Colonel R.B. Goodden. The inspection took place during August 1942.

been made. Messrs Rowe and Co would be fined 10s, including two guineas costs, and the assistant £1.

During late 1942, airfields in Cornwall were expanded to cope with the amount of troops and planes leaving the county in preparation of the Allied invasion of North Africa.

The *Western Morning News* of Friday, 4 September carried a story about how German raiders had killed patients at the Royal Cornwall Infirmary. The story stated that it could now be divulged that the South-West town which had suffered from a recent enemy air raid was, in fact, Truro. It was the first time it had experienced such action. Two planes, flying very low, dashed over the city at a terrific rate in the evening. They came from the west and travelled close to the housetops. One went right over the Royal Cornwall Infirmary, which in the last few years had been extended at a cost of £65,000. A bomb was dropped immediately before it reached the institution and pitched on the new portion of the building, a loud explosion following a second later, with large quantities of dust and debris rising to a considerable height. The bomb fell near to the new main entrance, which was wrecked, and the dispensary and the junction to the men's and women's wards was demolished. Fire broke out and burnt fiercely but the fire brigade quickly got the serious conflagration under control and within an hour and a half it was practically extinguished.

The infirmary was full with 200 patients and it was really remarkable that, considering the amount of the building demolished and the extent of the explosion, there were not more than eight deaths there. A good many were injured more or less severely. Members of the hospital staff, doctors and nurses, members of Civil Defence forces and many other willing helpers, including Home Guard and military, worked tremendously hard in evacuating the patients, who were removed to rest centres. The big task was accomplished before darkness set in, many ambulances and other vehicles being used for the purpose. There were nine deaths arising from the attack on the hospital. They were Sister Kathleen Peacock and Nurse Rachel Appleby, members of the hospital staff; Mrs Morley, of Leeds and her son, Private Fred Morley, a patient; Mr and Mrs P.A. Mortimore, who were visiting their child, who was also killed; Miss Mary Cicely Polglase, WAAF, and a baby named Skinner.

The other plane appeared at the same instant over the railway station with machine-gun and cannon fire and it came so low that it was able to fire under the platform roof and kill with cannonshot two men who were on the platform. They were Mr E. Pentecost, a postman, and Mr H.P. Williams, a railway employee. Continuing its violent and murderous way, machine-gunning as it went and injuring some people, it dropped a bomb in Agar Road, near the building which was formerly the Truro Diocesan Training College. Two persons were so severely injured that they later died including Mr S. Hooper, who resided at Agar Road, and Mr G.R. Gray, of St Mawes. A number of houses were partly wrecked and rendered uninhabitable, the glass of houses was broken over a wide area and many windows of St Paul's Church were smashed.

In one house, connected with a home which was badly damaged, there were fifteen persons, but only one was slightly injured. In another dwelling, a bed and cot, in which children were lying, were completely buried by debris, but the youngsters were rescued little the worse for their experience. Mrs Hooper was found sitting on the edge of a small crater, with her leg blown off. She succumbed but never made any complaint and behaved most pluckily. Mrs Edwards, whose house was also badly damaged, was telephoning at the time and did not hear the plane and the first thing she knew was that the place was coming down about her. Her husband was in the garage, which was machine-gunned, and he sustained a hand injury. Later it was found that a machine-gun bullet had gone through the pillow on his bed and entered the mattress.

Any desire on the part of the enemy to lessen the morale of citizens had little or no effect. There was certainly curiosity to see what damage had been done but that was all. Next morning, it was a case of carrying on as usual and there was a broadcast through the streets, issued with authority, that the situation created the previous evening had been effectively dealt with. One result of the event was to steel hearts towards avenging the murder of defenceless men, women and children. A most gratifying feature was the celerity with which the position at the Infirmary was cleaned up in very quick time and the mass of debris was cleared right away, and there were many willing helpers to make shipshape again the undamaged and inhabitable portions of the institution. Many women, some members of the WVS, brought their own pails and scrubbing brushes and worked with hearty goodwill, so that the hospital was open again for out-patients two days after the event, and very soon after that the readmission of in-patients was commenced. Seventy-three were returned in one day, and several thousands of pounds were subscribed towards a fund started to provide for the re-equipment of the infirmary.

In October, the Americans started using the airfield at St Eval to aid the anti-submarine forces. Consolidated B-24 Liberator bombers of the 409th Bombardment Squadron were deployed there from RAF Alconbury in Huntingdonshire.

march past of members of the rmy Cadet Force at Saltash uring October. They were spected by Colonel Fleming.

The *Cornishman* of Thursday, 8 October reported on the help that Cornwall was getting from the Red Cross. It stated that the many friends of Mr and Mrs Tom Goldsworthy, of Ingwenia, Carbis Bay, would congratulate them having heard through British Red Cross that their relatives in Jersey were not only alive but well. There had been a long silence since the Channel Islands were invaded by the Germans. Some people had escaped on the last boat, which was bombed, but many had neither been able to get letters nor money since the commandeering of their property. The families of Messrs Goldsworthy and White had long been connected with mining interests in Cornwall and overseas. Seventy years previously, Tom Goldsworthy, senior, had retired from Californian mines and settled in his home at Gwinear Churchtown. Mr Goldsworthy, junior, retired from the Transvaal many years before. He had his earlier engineering training with Messrs Harvey and Co at Hayle.

The late Major White's family had long been connected with South Africa and India and played a prominent part in the Levant mining area at St Just.

Some of the Jersey refugees stayed for some time in West Cornwall. News was still urgently needed of the fate of Cornish folk at Kuala Lumpur and other parts of Malaya.

Some civilians who were in Japan were known to have reached Lorenco Marques, en route to South Africa, Abyssinia and other destinations. News only filtered through to Cornwall at rare intervals from Unoccupied France, and this came via Portugal, with the aid of the Red Cross.

In November, the 1st Anti-submarine Squadron were deployed to St Eval from Langley Field in Virginia. Together with the 2nd Anti-submarine Squadron (which arrived in January 1943) they flew missions in long-range Liberator bombers equipped with Radar. From St Eval, the crews sort out German U-boats in the Bay of Biscay. In March 1943, the squadrons were reassigned to Port Lyautey in French Morocco.

The *Western Morning News* of Saturday, 7 November 1942 reported on Cornwall's part in victories abroad. It said that the Day of Remembrance in Cornwall would be observed this year in gratitude not only to those who gave their lives to defeat Germany and her Allies in the last war, but also to those who had given their all to the same end in the past three years.

More especially, of course, there would be deep gratitude and profound admiration for all the killed, the wounded and those unscathed who had given the people the great victory in the Western Desert.

It had been a triumph for all services and, although no specifically Cornish units had been mentioned among the regiments taking part in the land operations, men from the county were serving in all branches of the services in the Middle East and had doubtless contributed their small share to the gratifying results of the previous fortnight or so.

To the Royal Navy, whose share in the rout of Rommel had been sure, if unspectacular, Cornwall sent more sons, in proportion to population, than any other county in England.

But she had contributed many sons (and daughters also) to the army and the RAF, both of which the county had supported materially.

The contribution announced of over £1,300 from the people of the county to Army Welfare was a tidy sum from a first venture in flag-days and was symbolic of the solicitude of Cornish folk for the khaki men whom the war had brought into their midst. The same solicitude, particularly among their womenfolk, was shown by their devoted service in canteens, stationary and mobile, and in a variety of endeavours to make the army men and women feel at home.

Squadron Leader Sir John Molesworth-St Aubyn announced that there were now over 1,500 Cornish boys serving in the ranks of the ATC and there was an increased liaison between the corps and the RAF stations in Cornwall.

The *Western Morning News* of Thursday, 26 November reported that the honorable general secretary of the Cornish Association of the Transvaal, Johannesburg, had written to Lieutenant-Colonel E.H.W. Bolitho, Lord-Lieutenant for Cornwall, thanking him for his letter of 11 July, in which he acknowledged the receipt of a draft for £100. The writer added:

> We were very glad to learn that the enemy had not been visiting Cornwall too frequently but very much regret the more recent news that considerable damage had been caused in various parts of the county and that many lives had been lost. Our sympathy goes out to all those who've lost dear ones and we trust that there will be no repetition. We read with pride of the courage and bravery of nurses, the members of the fire services, the auxiliary services and the civilians. We will send a further draft for £50 for the benefit of those in Cornwall who suffer from enemy hands. With best wishes from all members of the Cornish Association of the Transvaal.

In the *Western Morning News* of Thursday, 3 December, mention was made of several people who were fined for selling and receiving clothing coupons. The story stated that several charges of dealing in clothing coupons, the first of their kind in West Cornwall, were heard on the previous day by the West Penwith magistrates. Mrs Catherine Ellen Davies, of 33 Trelawney Place, Hayle, was charged with transferring clothing coupons to Mrs Rosemary Tonkin, 58, of Mount Pleasant Road, Camborne, and she was charged with being in possession of coupons issued to another person. Both defendants pleaded 'Guilty.' Mr Hancock (Truro), who prosecuted on behalf of the Board of Trade, said the department and the police were rather concerned with the prevalence of offences of this kind in Hayle.

The traffic in coupons struck at the root of the rationing system and the Board of Trade took a very serious view of the offence. They regarded the purchase of coupons as the more serious, because it enabled a person who was better off to get extra coupons from poorer people who could not resist the temptation of selling the coupons which they could not use themselves.

Mrs Davies said she asked Mrs Tonkin whether she wanted any clothing coupons as she had several to spare and they were of no use her. Nothing was paid for them as she was on Public Assistance and had no money to spend on clothing. Mrs Tonkin corroborated this statement and said she used the coupons to purchase clothes for her wedding. She did not know it was an offence to receive coupons, although she knew it was an offence to buy them. There was a further charge against Mrs Davies of transferring coupons, to Mr Thomas George Hosking, of Hayle, and he was charged with being in possession of coupons issued to another person. Mr Hosking, who was represented by Mr Eric Thomas (Penzance), pleaded 'Guilty.' In this case, Mrs Davies said she gave Hosking the clothing coupons which she could not use on the understanding that she was given some second-hand clothing. Mr Hosking gave her 4s for them. Mr Thomas said his client now realized what a foolish thing he had done. He had been a good friend to Mrs Davies, but in this case he was tempted by the chance of getting extra clothing coupons and fell.

Hosking was fined £2 and Mrs Davies and Mrs Tonkin £1 each.

The *Western Morning News* of Thursday, 31 December carried a story about gifts to soldiers in hospital. It stated that the Cornwall Red Cross and St John Joint War Committee had sent Christmas gifts of cheques to thirty-five hospitals and sick quarters in Cornwall to help brighten the Christmas for those who, owing to illness, had to spend their time laid up. Many grateful letters had been received, including one which stated:

> In spite of present difficulties, I have been able to purchase refreshments, cigarettes and chocolates, which helped considerably brighten the Christmas of those who, through sickness, were prevented from joining in the festivities normally arranged to make Christmas as happy a time as possible for the troops.

CHAPTER FIVE

1943 – Over here!

The *Western Morning News* of Friday, 1 January carried a congratulation for Cornwall's salvage teams.

'There is a great deal to congratulate ourselves upon,' remarked the Lord-Lieutenant at Truro at a meeting of the Executive Committee to wind up the Cornwall County salvage drive, which took place between 19 September and 3 October. He added that no doubt the drive was fully justified and was helpful to the nation's needs. Mr L.P. New (secretary) presented a return showing that the drive target for the county for the fortnight was 586 tons but the actual record was 854 tons. In almost every case, the drive figures showed advances over the fortnightly average for the three months to July. In one instance, it was 1,161 per cent, and in another 979. It was difficult to draw comparisons between one authority and another because of their differences in character. Some areas did not obtain such successful results during the drive as others and that was because of their intensive efforts over a period, instead of the period of the drive only. St Ives Borough, Saltash Borough and Camelford Rural did not take part in the drive.

The director of Salvage and Recovery wrote that the drive showed what could be done by intensive effort even after three years of war.

'We are now,' he said, 'experiencing a serious drop in the salvage figures, particularly as regards waste paper, metals and kitchen waste for feeding-stuffs and it is more necessary than ever to urge local authorities to do everything in their power to improve their collection of these materials.'

During 1943, a mock seaborne raid codenamed 'Exercise Brandyball' took place at the 'Brandys' on the cliffs close to Bosigran on the Land's End peninsula. The exercise involved No 4 British Commando.

As part of the scrap metal drive, children helped by contributing whatever they could find.

A worker sorting out scrap metal which had been collected in the recent campaign. Tons of food tins were collected each week.

Waste paper being unloaded from a barge. There was a shortage of paper and it was rationed from September 1939. Newspapers were only allowed to use so much so some editions weren't printed.

Scrap metal being sorted out ready to be melted down. Thousands of meat boxes were rescued from people's dustbins.

The *Western Morning News* of Wednesday, 20 January reported on the proposal to have women police in Cornwall.

By an overwhelming majority, Cornwall Standing Joint Committee at Bodmin on the previous Monday adhered to its decision not to appoint women police for patrol duties.

A resolution from a conference at Truro, representative of societies dealing with moral and welfare work in the city, reaffirmed its strong conviction of the urgent need for the appointment of fully trained women police to act as ordinary patrolling constables.

Mr W.T. Hart said that when the report of the conference was published, his attention was called to the statement that over a hundred clergymen signed the petition supporting the appeal to the committee. They were all conversant with the point continuously being stressed that women police would act from a social welfare point of view rather than in connection with contravention of the law. It had occurred to some of them that if the clergymen of the city were to exercise their influence as well as preaching their sermons on Sundays they might accomplish something to obviate what was happening in the county.

The chairman (Mr A. Browning Lyne) said he had never held the view that there was no case for the appointment of women police in Cornwall. He had questioned whether there was sufficient cause to justify the appointment but he did think a case of a sort, subject to a lot of qualifications, could be made out for the appointment of some women police in Cornwall, particularly in present times.

He knew it meant a substantial cost to the county, because it was just as well to leave the matter alone if they were only going to appoint three or four. If they had three or four points in the county for control, it must mean at least two women at each point, so that they were entitled to ask themselves whether they considered Cornwall was justified in bearing that expenditure.

Mr T. Blamey said that having regard to the bodies represented and the way the subject had been brought before the committee, there was no doubt they were trying to force women police on the county. The chairman had referred to the public opinion represented at the conference but at least 95 per cent of the people of Rowland, which he represented, were very much against women police.

Mr Noel Purcell contended there was enough money among the societies represented at the conference to engage women workers to do the work required of them under the control of the societies themselves. These people wanted to foist women police on the chief constable to replace the constables they had and interfere with the force. He proposed the committee adhere to its previous resolution and suggest to the societies that they should employ their own people for the duties they expected women police to do.

Seconding, Mr Hart said, after investigations, they had found that the expense would be colossal.

Moving the appointment of six women police, Mr C.M. Knowles said the powers of women police were the same as male. Women policemen in uniforms had a moral and legal authority that the ordinary welfare worker did not possess.

The promoters of the movement had undoubtedly presented a formidable case. The time had come to say that in the absence of such a reasoned case by the opposers to the appointment, the committee had no choice but to accede to the request of the promoters of that movement and appoint women police.

Mr J.M. Finlay seconded on the assumption that it was purely an emergency proposal.

The chairman suggested the amendment should be altered to appoint a committee to receive a report from the chief constable as to the possibilities of getting suitable women, their training and accommodation, and the probable cost to the county.

On this amendment being put, only the chairman, the proposer and seconder voted for it and the resolution was carried. Presenting the annual estimates, Mr F.R. Woodward said there was a reduction in the cost on the rates of £1,495, due entirely to the reduction in the amount of pay of the men going into the forces and the substitution of War Reserves, whose pay was met by the Home Office.

The chairman referred to the agreement which had been reached between the Penzance Borough Council and the Standing Joint Committee over the suggested amalgamation of the police forces, but said nothing could be published at that stage as the terms had not been approved by the Home Office.

It was agreed that the clerk should publish the details as soon as the Home Office approval had been received.

In February, RAF Trebulzue was enlarged and had two concrete

2

Freepost Plus RTKE-RGRJ-KTTX
Pen & Sword Books Ltd
47 Church Street
BARNSLEY
S70 2AS

DISCOVER MORE ABOUT MILITARY HISTORY

Pen & Sword Books have over 4000 books currently available, our imprints include; Aviation, Naval, Military, Archaeology, Transport, Frontline, Seaforth and the Battleground series, and we cover all periods of history on land, sea and air.

Keep up to date with our new releases by completing and returning the form below (no stamp required if posting in the UK).

Alternatively, if you have access to the internet, please complete your details online via our website at **www.pen-and-sword.co.uk.**

All those subscribing to our mailing list via our website will receive a free e-book, *Mosquito Missions* by Martin W Bowman. Please enter code number ACC1 when subscribing to receive your free e-book.

Mr/Mrs/Ms ....

Address ....

Postcode.................... Email address...

Website: www.pen-and-sword.co.uk Email: enquiries@pen-and-sword.co.uk
Telephone: 01226 734555 Fax: 01226 734438
Stay in touch: facebook.com/penandswordbooks or follow us on Twitter @penswordbooks

runways added. Its name was changed to RAF St Mawgan and it was used to transport aircraft to Africa.

News of flower racketeers appeared in the *Sunday Mirror* of Sunday, 21 February. The article stated that flower racketeers had found a new dodge to beat the transport restrictions. Since trains were barred to them after the *Sunday Pictorial* first exposed their game, they had started using buses. The racketeers filled suitcases and took them on buses, which was perfectly legal. Exposure of the Cornwall Express flower racket had not completely deterred the railway black marketeers, however. They were still trying to sneak suitcases full to London. Two of them were caught at Reading on the previous day and were fined £5 and £2 for taking three suitcases of violets and daffodils by train from Cornwall. The flowers had been sent to local hospitals.

Not all had their minds on the war as a letter to the *Western Morning News* of Saturday, 27 February showed. It read:

Sir, -

In view of Mr R Glave Saunders being surprised at the reawakening of his tortoise from its long winter sleep a month earlier than usual, it will interest him and others to know that two tortoises in my garden have not hibernated at all this season but have been out and about all through the winter.

C H STEPHENS. Breage, Helston, Feb. 25.

The *Western Morning News* of Tuesday, 2 March carried a story about the Land Army in Cornwall. A reporter wrote:

Following my first article on the Women's Land Army in Devon, I naturally turned to Cornwall for the second and Mrs Charles Williams (chairman of the Cornwall Committee of the WLA) was able to give me details of conditions in that county.

Several women signing up to help with agricultural work at a local farm.

Commenting that although there are about 1,000 girls working in Cornwall, she said 300 more are wanted immediately. Over 100 farmers are waiting for Land Army girls, and a large number of them are also wanted for employment with the War Agricultural Committee. At present, there are very few openings for girls in horticultural spheres, most of the farmers wanting them to do milking. In this the girls are given especially careful training of at least one month's duration. During this period of training, in addition to being given money for their board and lodging, they are paid pocket money of 10s weekly.

Of these 1,000 girls working in the county, the bulk are on private farms. In Cornwall, the farms generally speaking, are not very large, and consequently the girls are wanted mainly for general work, not to specialize. A good number are engaged in rat-catching, three different methods being employed, and they go around in vans with all the necessary props for this job.

In Cornwall, as in Devon, there are 'gang' workers, and consequently hostels have to be run for them. There are four in West Cornwall, run by the YWCA, with experienced wardens in charge who look after the welfare of the girls, and in the next few months it is hoped to have a hostel in every district in the county. At present, there are three in the Penzance neighbourhood, and either at the end of March or in April, it is hoped to open another to accommodate 130 girls.

When I mentioned to Mrs Williams the recent criticism of the Land Army being insufficiently disciplined and controlled, her very prompt reply was, 'The Land Army is unfortunately named. From the word Army, people think it is a Service.'

She added that as the other women's services had suffered, so had the WLA in shortage of uniforms. Now, owing to restrictions, very few girls can be supplied with gum boots. Instead they are issued with two pairs of leather boots and gaiters. There has been the suggestion that clogs may be given for dairy work, but nothing definite on this subject has yet been decided.

In the Penzance district, when the peak period of lifting potatoes arrives in June, it is expected there will be between 600 and 700 workers in that area alone. Of course, they will not

Driver H. Glasson of Penzance and Driver T. Sowden of Redruth who were both reported well in the Cornishman of Thursday 18 March 1943. Both were serving in the Middle East.

all be Land Army girls, the deficiency in numbers being made up by other classes of workers. Mrs Williams told me that two new training centres had recently been opened, both of which were being conducted by highly-experienced dairy experts. The one at Colonel Bolitho's Home Farm, at Trengwainton, near Penzance, is in the charge of Miss Jane Olde, and the other, situated near St. Erth, under Miss Dora Nicholas. Miss Ann Bolitho, daughter of the Lord-Lieutenant for Cornwall, was, it will be remembered, one of the two Land Army girls from Cornwall who went to London for inspection by the Queen in 1940.

The majority of the girls are billeted where they work, or else in a nearby village, and once a month every girl is visited by her district representative, there being one in each part of the county.

During March, it was reported that a Devon and Cornwall Club had been formed at a prisoner of war camp in Germany which had fifty-six members. The president was SSM C.W. Davis, RASC and the secretary was L/Sergeant W.E. Richards, RA.

In a letter home, the secretary stated that the main objectives of the club were:

1. To enable men from the same town or district to meet and, if unknown to each other, to become acquainted.

2. To meet for the exchange and discussion of news from the two counties.

3. To promote social activities.

4. Mutual assistance.

5. To keep a record of prisoners from the two counties in order to

facilitate the arranging of reunions on their return to the United Kingdom.

The *Cornishman* of Thursday, 8 April reported on West Cornwall Wings Week. It stated that no stone would be left unturned to ensure the success of the Penzance, West and St Just Wings for Victory Week from June 19 to 26 inclusive. The target was quarter of a million pounds and it was hoped that the total may reach the £300,000 mark. It was interesting to note in that respect that Truro, the openers of the Week in Cornwall, reached £277,000. It was felt that what Truro could do, so could Penzance.

A meeting of the Publicity Committee for the Week, held at the Municipal buildings on the previous Friday evening, went a good way towards deciding on the form of the parade on the opening day. 'It was hoped that this would be the biggest parade ever,' said Mr W.J. Hichens (the honorary General Secretary), presiding in the enforced absence of the chairman, Alderman John Birch, JP.

Plans for the parade were discussed under the direction of the Honorary Campaign Secretary and all of the Services, Civil Defence and other representatives present, unhesitatingly signifying their intention of seeing to it that contingents were provided to make a mammoth procession.

Among the bands it was hoped would participate were those of the Royal Marines (Plymouth), the Durham LI, the South Lancs and possibly from the Royal Air Force, the Home Guard, the RA and Camborne Town.

Prominent in the procession, were to be contingents from the RAF and the WAAF, whilst it was hoped that there would be representative numbers from the Royal Navy and the WRNS, the Merchant Navy, the Royal Artillery Coast Battery and light AA (both of these with guns), the DCLI, RAF Cadets, Home Guards in strength from the whole of West Cornwall, Sea Cadets, Army Cadet Force and Air Training Corps, police and special police, Civil Defence services, St John Ambulance and Cadets, RNLI, Coastguards and Royal Observer Corps, Red Cross, WVS, NFS. Women's Land Army, Girls' Training Corps and many others. Transport would be the determining factor in many cases.

One special attraction would be the appearance, which it was hoped would be possible, of members of the United States Army and Army Air Force.

Since everything possible was being done to ensure the success of the Week at Hayle and St Just, as well as at Penzance, separate parades would be held at those places mid-week, so that some contingents from Hayle and St Just might elect to go in their own processions, though there would be nothing to stop them appearing in both.

There would, it was hoped, be lorries with guns and other weapons, tableaux, and so forth.

Arrangements were also being made for a visit by a Sunderland flying boat.

The questions of the marshal for the parade, and also of the route to be taken, were still open, but the latter would probably be from the Eastern Green, up Market Jew Street, along Alverton and down Alexandra Road.

The first American GIs (29th Division) arrived in Cornwall in May 1943.

American troops were stationed near Looe and Liskeard. Amongst them, was a battalion of black troops who were billeted at Doublebois House.

Black and white US troops were given separate nights off so that they wouldn't come into contact with each other. Locals welcomed the troops but there was some dismay from the white Americans when English girls were seen with black GIs. The Red Cross in Truro was obliged to supply two separate clubs, one for white and one for black soldiers. When the two groups met, there were fist fights, stabbings and even shootings.

A black singer, John Payne, was invited to the home of Lady Cook, in Talland, near Looe, to escape the Blitz in London. When the Americans arrived in Cornwall, Payne made contact with the black soldiers and formed a choir.

At the beginning of May, the *Western Morning News* carried a story about Cornwall's ATC. It stated that six months of hard work and steady progress was reported to the Cornwall County Committee of the Air Training Corps at their meeting at Truro on the previous day by Sir John Molesworth-St Aubyn, the district inspecting officer.

He said the six months had been a testing time for the movement.

No new squadrons had been formed but Camborne had started an extremely successful new naval flight which was doing very well.

They had lost 100 cadets, which was not as serious as it looked when it was remembered that there was a steady drift of evacuated boys returning back to their homes. Also, it was only natural that, in spite of their very friendly co-operation with the Army Cadet Force, this movement should make some difference.

He believed, however, they were around the corner and that already numbers were picking up, which, in view of the very urgent need of the RAF for air recruits was most important.

They had recently been fortunate in that the Air Ministry had sent a plane to Cornwall especially to fly cadets and during the course of this visit 300 cadets were flown. This did more good than anything in keeping up the enthusiasm of the cadets.

The total number of cadets in the county was 1,559. The Isles of Scilly had twenty-one proficient cadets out of twenty-two, which was a record for the country and very creditable.

During May, William L. Brooks of 15 Egloshayle Road, Wadebridge, objected to military service on the grounds that he couldn't take a life. He didn't appear in court due to illness but was represented by his wife and mother. In a written statement, he said that he had applied for full-time service in the NFS but had been refused owing to his medical grading. The tribunal was not satisfied that a case of conscientious objection had been established within the meaning of the act and the application was dismissed.

Meanwhile, Arthur Cloke, a mason of 30 Commercial Road, Hayle, quoted the commandment, 'Thou shall not kill.' His honour Judge Wethered, presiding, told him that this was a perversion of the word of God. Cloke, a baptist, declared that it was impossible to defeat evil with evil. God did not create men to destroy one another.

Judge Wethered said that by his attitude he was helping the Germans to kill his family. He was taking all the benefits of living in this country and repudiating all the obligations.

Cloke was retained on the register and marked for service in the non-combatant corps.

During the second half of 1943 and the first half of 1944, thousands

Rows of Nissan huts provided accommodation for the many American servicemen stationed in Cornwall.

A religious service given for the American servicemen within a converted Nissan hut.

American troops helping out wherever they could. Many helped people who had been bombed out of their homes and they also helped with the clearing up of debris.

of American troops occupied Devon and Cornwall complete with vehicles and equipment.

Americans arrived at St Mawgan airbase during June. The 491st Base and Air Base Squadron of USAAF Air Transport Command made the post their home and worked together with the No. 2 Overseas Aircraft Despatch Unit of the RAF. It soon became one of the busiest bases in Great Britain with extensive movements between Britain and America as well as to North Africa and later, the Far East.

The *Western Morning News* of Saturday, 19 June carried a story about Wings Week. It mentioned that one of the surprises in the 'Wings for Victory' campaign in mid-Cornwall the previous week was the amount that Mevagissey raised.

Final figures showed that £17,575 was taken. Mr A.L. Tucker, the honorary secretary of the 'Wings' Committee, stated that Mevagissey had done well in the previous two national subscriptions but the Wings effort 'tops the lot.' Although the drums had not been beaten much to arouse enthusiasm, Mevagissey had gone about the job in a quiet way and had even surprised itself.

During June, American army lorry drivers were taught the British Highway Code. Many of the US trucks were too wide for the country roads.

Also in June, the US Army Air Forces took over RAF Trebulzue where they carried out major improvements. These included building a new control tower and an extension of the main runway. During the latter part of 1943, it became one of the most used airfields in Britain.

Mr W.F.A. Bell, the local representative of Cable and Wireless Ltd, handing to the mayor of Penzance (Alderman E.C. Harvey) confirmation of the company's investment of £100,000 in Penzance, St Just and Penwith's 'Wings for Victory' Week.

During July, HRH the Duchess of Gloucester visited Cornwall. She is pictured with Colonel W. Blackwood, the county commissioner of St John and chairman of the joint war committee. T. are seen outside the Moresk Drill Hall i Truro.

The *Cornishman* of Thursday, 8 July told of Cornish prisoners of war. It stated that the cost to the War Organization of the Red Cross and St John to feed prisoners of war from Cornwall was over £18,000 a year. The Cornwall Joint War Committee hoped very much that Cornwall might be able to contribute very largely towards this cost, in addition to the magnificent response which had been made in the county to the three national appeals, i.e. Penny-a-Week, Flag Day and the Agriculture Fund. An appeal was therefore made in March, known as the Cornwall

Independence Day in Cornwall on 4 July 1943. The Stars and Stripes and the Infantry Banner can be seen passing the saluting base during the Independence Day parade.

Prisoners of War Food Parcel Fund, and a most generous response had been made. All donations received were forwarded each month to the Duke of Gloucester's Fund. In April £244 2s 9d was sent, in May £568 7s 4d and in June £723 9s 11d, making a total of £1,536.

Bob Hope entertaining American troops at Bodmin during July 1943.

During July, 1943, Bob Hope travelled to Cornwall and entertained the American troops stationed at Bodmin. His shows and appearances proved very popular and boosted the morale of the men.

The *Western Morning News* of Monday, 19 July discussed savings in Cornwall. An announcement was made at the Cornwall county conference of the National Savings Committee at Truro that while small savings over the country in 'Wings for Victory' Weeks were £3 18s per head, the figure for Cornwall was £6 2s 7d.

The mayor (Alderman W.J. Kemp) welcomed the delegates and Mr P.G. Heppenstall, the regional member who deputized for Sir Harold Mackintosh, and as chairman, congratulated Cornwall on the magnificent result of the schools effort and said the scheme for the autumn campaign was partly based on their work. There was an enormous contribution in small savings in the Wings Weeks.

Mr E.C.H. Jones, assistant secretary of the National Committee, brought the congratulations of Lord Kindersley and the National Committee to Cornwall for their outstanding performance in savings in recent years. Whatever loose talk there might be, finance remained the foundation of the economic and industrial structure and the work of the Savings Committees would remain to be done under much more difficult conditions when the war was over.

Those who had turned their hand to this work during the war should not give it up until they were satisfied the nation no longer needed their services.

The Regional Commissioner for National Savings (Mr E.H. Harwood) reported that the number of savings groups in the region had risen from 2,957 on March 31 1939 to 15,321 on March 31 1942, and a further increase during this year to 17,724. Street groups had increased during the past year from 5,112 to 7,756. A great deal of attention had been directed during the year to improving the position of groups in large firms. There had been a marked rise in the monthly savings per employee in these firms in April and May owing to the incidence of Wings Weeks, no less than 28s per head in April and to 26s in May. During the preceding twelve months, the figure ranged between 8s 9d and 12s 10d.

The position in the smaller firms was less satisfactory, the average monthly subscription per employee being rather less than 9s per head.

Cedric Drewe, MP and Parliamentary Private Secretary the Minister of Agriculture, presenting the National Victory urn to Mr J. Lionel Rogers, Chairman of the Cornwall War Agricultural Executive Committee, who received it on behalf of the county at a presentation ceremony at Truro during July 1943.

Sales of Savings Certificates showed an increase for 1940 of 140 per cent over the 1939 figures, for 1941 an increase of 273 per cent over 1940, and for 1942 an increase of 54 per cent over 1941. The cash value of Savings Certificates sold in the region for 1943 was £13,372,226. Net deposit figures in the Post Office Savings Banks increased from £10,382,083 for the year ending March, 1942, to £10,869,411 for the year ending March, 1943, while net deposits in the Trustee Savings Banks advanced from £2,192,487 to £2,906,705.

Mr Harwood expressed thanks to the voluntary workers in Cornwall and said that they could not have had a more public-spirited or hard-working body. The *Western Morning News* of Thursday, 22 July reported on Youth Camps in the county. It mentioned that Cornwall Youth Camp, under the auspices of Cornwall County Council, had been the scene of much youthful activity during the previous weekends and had as visitors on July 17 and 18 a platoon of the Army Cadet Corps from Camborne, under the command of Cadet-Lieutenant W.G. Westcott. Cadets brought their own rations and the general domestic arrangements of the camp were under the guidance of the County Youth organizer, Cadet-Captain Warren-Wren.

A Whitley and Liberator bomber collided on the runway at St Eval during August 1943. The Whitley was carrying depth charges which caught fire, causing a massive explosion which killed both crews outright.

The *Cornishman* of Thursday, 26 August issued an appeal to readers to help with the forthcoming Saturday's Aid to Russia Flag Day. It stated that on the forthcoming Saturday in Cornwall, a flag day would take place to support Mrs Churchill and her Aid to Russia Fund for medical supplies for our gallant Allies. The newspaper stated that the Soviet army was

One of three semi-mobile kitchens in action. They were presented to Cornwall by the Ministry of Food during July.

During August 1943, a garden show was held at the police headquarters in Bodmin. Policemen gardeners from all over the county sent contributions. About £33 was raised for Bodmin District Nursing Association.

'on the crest of a wave,' but their losses were tremendous. Adequate medical supplies would prevent many of the wounded cases from becoming fatalities.

The *Cornishman* continued by saying that the Russians had shown unbelievable stoicism and grit in their fight against the Nazi threat. Helped by supplies from America and ourselves, they had been enabled to stand at bay to wear down the mighty German hordes. It was reported that now they had taken the offensive, Cornwall must go on helping, supporting the fund of Mrs Churchill.

Between September 1943 and April 1944, Tregantle Fort, near Torpoint, received visits from the American boxers, Joe Louis, Jackie Wilson and Sugar Ray Robinson.

The *Cornishman* of Thursday, 2 September reported on how Cornwall was aiding the Red Cross. The newspaper stated that through the popular Red Cross Penny-a-Week Fund, the people of Cornwall were giving invaluable help to the Red Cross and St John, which was doing such splendid work at home and overseas. To the end of July, residents in the county had contributed no less than £35,494 to the fund. Of this £24,036, came from house-to-house collections in the principal urban centres, whilst no less than £11,458 was contributed at their place of employment by men and women workers of 246 firms and organizations.

An average of £85,000 was being raised every week by some 12 million contributors to the Penny-a-Week Fund throughout the country.

Margaret Hawke, aged 11, of Gustiveor, St Columb Minor near Newquay, showing how well she can handle a team of horses. She worked by herself and harrowed many acres.

An ATS birthday parade in Cornwall during September 1943. A contingent of the ATS can be seen marching past the saluting base in Truro. The celebration marked the fifth anniversary of the organization. The Area Commander took the salute.

The *Western Morning News* of Wednesday, 22 September carried a story about a Make-do and Mend exhibition. It stated that some indication of the keen interest shown in the visit of the Make-do and Mend exhibition, sponsored by Cornwall Education Committee, to Wadebridge, may be gathered from the fact that during the first two hours it was open, it was visited by upwards of 500 people.

The exhibition which had already been to various Cornish towns showed striking examples of what could be done in the direction of mending and renovations, household jobbery, patchwork and fuel saving. Demonstrations were also given in wartime cooking.

The *Western Morning News* of Tuesday, 5 October reported on a disturbance in Cornwall caused by US soldiers. European Headquarters stated that on the previous night, twenty-one American soldiers, arrested after a shooting fracas with United States Army military policemen on September 26 in Cornwall, were being held pending an investigation by the United States Army Provost Marshal.

The two wounded military policemen were under treatment at a United States Army hospital.

At about 10.00 pm on the previous Sunday, September 26 a few pedestrians and residents around the usually quiet square of a Cornish town were startled by the chattering of guns and the sound of shouting. Shooting, in which a number soldiers were involved, went on for a few minutes until the arrival of a force of American military police. None of the civilians were hurt but two American military policemen were wounded, one seriously.

Mr Walter Rail on Nosey Parker taking a jump at a rodeo in Bodmin during September 1943.

Windows of houses in the vicinity bore traces of the affray. Holes were found in many of them and one bullet had penetrated a lath and plaster wall of an old shop.

Apparently, the men had broken camp and secured guns and come into town bent on trouble.

On the Friday, several American high-ranking officers, including Generals, visited the town and conducted an investigation. Photographs of the square were taken and an immobilized car, which was standing in the square and which was apparently in the way, was removed bodily by twenty men and replaced after the pictures had been taken.

On Friday, 8 October, at Penzance Quarter Sessions, Edward Butler and Harry Moore, two privates of the Devonshire Regiment, were charged with breaking and entering the jeweller's shop of H.A. Williams of Penzance and stealing sixty-four watches.

Another soldier of the same regiment, Charles Huggins, was charged with receiving the watches knowing them to have been stolen. Henry Baker, a motor engineer, was charged with receiving two of the watches.

After a hearing which lasted all day, Huggins and Baker were found guilty on all charges. Baker, who was thought to be the worst offender, was sentenced to 16 months in prison and Butler and Huggins were sentenced to 6 months. It was decided to give Moore another chance and he was fined £5 and bound over for 12 months.

On Saturday, 16 October, Flight Officer William James Croft, serving in the RAF, was brought before the court at Helston charged with murdering Joan Nora Lewis, a corporal in the WAAF, aged 26, who was a native of Porthcawl, Wales. She was found dead in a summer house with two bullet wounds.

The *Western Morning News* reported that it was understood that the couple had been very friendly and the woman was being transferred to another section on the Saturday. A service revolver was found in the summer house.

Flight Officer Croft, aged 33, was a married man with two children, and had previously lived in Bath.

The *Western Morning News* of Monday, 18 October carried a story concerning an army absentee fined at Camelford.

Private Charles Earnest Mascall, of Dunheved Bungalow, Tintagel stated, 'I have a clean record in civilian life and 18 years' good conduct in the services,' when he appeared at Camelford on the previous Saturday when he pleaded 'Guilty' to obtaining 8s by means of larceny by trick.

Superintendent W.H. Mallett, of Launceston, said the defendant failed to return to his unit after his leave. On 6 October, he visited St Teath, where he was not known, and called on several persons, producing a scarf and a pair of gloves, together with numbered pieces of paper. He said the two articles were going to be raffled at the White Hart Hotel, St Teath, that evening, and the defendant sold the slips for 1s each. The proceeds, he said, would be for the wounded of the Eighth Army. No arrangements had been made for the raffle.

Defendant was fined £2, with £1 11s 4d costs, and was detained to await military escort.

During November, RAF St Mawgan was occupied by two USAAF Meteorology Flights. Between November 1943 and November 1944, BOAC operated limited scheduled services via St Mawgan.

The *Western Morning News* of Saturday, 6 November spoke of Anglo-American relations. It stated that as an addition to the measures which were being taken by Cornish people to entertain American forces stationed in the South West, Mrs Beatrice Wright, the MP for Bodmin, had suggested to the mayors in her constituency that public rooms should be made available for discussions and demonstrations of Cornish industries and characteristics and participation in Cornish singing.

Mrs Wright proposed that a list be compiled of those willing to give hospitality and that certain evenings in the week should be set aside when a reception committee would be present to entertain the visitors in a local hall or institute.

In this way, the Americans could gain an interest in the activities of the county and those who wished to entertain the visitors in their own homes would have an opportunity of becoming acquainted with their guests in advance.

Mrs Wright, who was herself of American birth, was anxious to ensure that if organized hospitality was developed, it would prove not only successful but of real value to greater Anglo-American understanding.

During November, the American 254th Engineer Combat Battalion were sent to Newquay.

Also, during December, Pentewan Beach was used for training by US naval units.

The paper shortage meant that no Christmas decorations were available in shops but people made do with improvised decorations made with recycled items.

The *Western Morning News* of Thursday, 30 December recapped on Cornwall's war effort during 1943. It stated that Cornwall's chief interest during the past year had been the winning of the war and all who had not joined the forces had been doing their bit.

The main industries had been carrying on as far as war conditions had permitted and, apart from their ordinary avocations, the civilian population had been continuing their war efforts to the very full.

One of the most satisfactory features had been the way which agriculturists had responded to the call of the government in respect of cultivation orders. They had done exceptionally well in putting 365,000 acres under the plough during the year, as compared with 248,000 during the previous year. This was more than was asked of them and they had been specially thanked by the Minister of Agriculture, who had quoted Cornwall as an example to other counties.

Unfortunately, they were not rewarded as they deserved, for conditions were such that 1943 was said to have been one of the most disastrous years for Cornish farming. All corn crops grew too fast and consequently weakly, so that they were badly laid. Rust set in on oats and dredge corn, with the result that both cereals were so poor that in lots of cases it was not worth the cost of threshing.

Wheat was also not good yielding, owing to lack of sun and dull weather, and samples were small and light. Thousands of acres were not saved at all owing to the weather.

A fairly good lot of hay was saved in the early part of the summer. There was an abundance of grass and mangolds. Swedes, kale etc. were above the average. Next season's wheat had been mostly planted and was up and looked very strong and well.

Another feature of the year was the raising of the agricultural wage from 48s to £3 a week and later going up still further to 65s. Contributions to the Red Cross Agriculture Fund had been exceedingly gratifying. As much as £27,292 was raised during the year making a total of £55,828 in three years. Truro district headed the year's contributions with £5,000. Launceston came next with £3,625 and Callington was commended for £2,485.

In the campaign for increased milk production, Cornwall won the silver victory churn, obtaining higher points than any of the English counties, the increase being 4,000,000 gallons over the previous year.

In regard to tin mining, there had been no great development or discovery and the industry had proceeded along humdrum but orderly lines, under government control. The three producing mines had been winning as much metal as possible having regard to available labour. The government had assisted by supplying additional labour but the art of getting tin could not be acquired in a short while, and the benefit of the imported extra labour would not yet be felt. The year's work had been of normal character. There was plenty of tin still left in the county and more could be obtained given more expert tin miners.

The fishing season had compared favourably with 1942. Pilchards were disappointing at first but the scanty returns of the earlier months were made up later and the controlled price enabled fishermen to make a better profit than appeared probable during the earlier days.

The china clay industry was considerably handicapped again through war conditions. There were few shipments abroad and home consumption was at about the same level. The total output was below 20 per cent of pre-war production.

The 'Wings for Victory' weeks resulted in £3,466,163 being raised, Penzance leading the way with £535,228, St Austell being second with £372,871 and Camborne third with £362,504. The total of the three major campaigns was £9,108,620 and the average small savings per head of the population was £6 2s, being considerably higher than that of the national.

The only political changes in the county had been in the Penryn-Falmouth Division. Mr A.L. Rewse, Labour candidate, resigned in June and Mr Percy Harris, Foxhole, was adopted as prospective Liberal candidate in October.

Distinguished visitors to the county included the Duchess of Gloucester, who in July inspected convalescent homes, Red Cross and St John workers and depots in Penzance, Truro, Newquay and other places.

Gross expenditure for the year in connection with the County

Council was estimated at £2,124,434 and by a majority of ten votes, it was decided to make a rate of 9s 6d in the £, as against a higher sum recommended by the Finance Committee.

In the matter of women police, the Standing Joint Committee had remained firm in their refusal to make appointments in spite of continued agitation and, at the last meeting of the County Council, it was decided by two votes not to send to the committee a resolution passed at a previous meeting advocating the urgent need for the appointment of fully-trained and attested women police to act as ordinary patrolling constables.

Anxiety had been expressed by local authorities in Cornwall regarding suggested reform of local government and reconstruction and, early in the year, an association was formed of local authorities for the protection of their interests.

During the year, St Ives revived the question of a harbour refuge for the north coast of Cornwall, the idea being that it should form part of a reconstruction programme after the war. St Ives put forward a claim to their having the most suitable site, and Padstow followed with the renewed proposal that that place should be selected.

Friends of the Royal Cornwall Infirmary, formed three years previously, reported a membership of 11,000, with numbers still growing. Three Cornishmen received honours from the King. The Lord-Lieutenant and chairman of the County Council (Lieutenant-Colonel E.H.W. Bolitho) received the CB in the New Year Honours List and Mr Noel E. Purcell (vice-chairman of the County Council) and Mr J. Wilson (executive officer of Cornwall War Agricultural Committee) were later in the year awarded the OBE.

CHAPTER SIX

1944 – D Day

During 1944, a wing at Prideaux Place became home to the 121st Engineer Combat Battalion of the US Army.

The *Western Morning News* of Friday, 7 January carried a report of an attack on a convoy off the coast of Cornwall. The article told how the German News Agency claimed, on the previous day, a major success by German MTBs against a convoy off the coast of Cornwall on the Wednesday night: 'They sank, without loss to themselves, five ships, totalling 12,500 tons, and one escort vessel,' the Agency said. The MTBs broke off the engagement only after the last torpedo had been fired and returned to base without damage, it added.

German Radio, giving details of the 'naval encounters' off the Cornish Coast, claimed: 'For the first time in this war, German speed boats went close into the South-West Coast of England, where they so surprised a convoy of steamers and escort ships that none of them could offer any serious defence.'

The Radio declared that the attack occurred between Land's End and the Lizard somewhat east of the Scilly Isles, at 3.00 am on the previous day. The Radio claimed that a 3,000-ton tanker, two 3,000-ton ships, a 2,000-ton vessel and one of about 1,500-tons, were sunk. The attack, it was stated, was made under the command of Captain Mueller.

Hundreds of American soldiers were stationed at Threemilestone, near Truro in a restricted area in preparation for D Day. Both white and black soldiers were stationed in the same camp and they were very friendly and well-loved by locals. The servicemen gave people sweets, tinned fruit and tinned soup, which they were happy to share. Some of the soldiers visited families' homes and dated local girls.

The *Western Daily Press* of Tuesday, 11 January reported that invasion armies were gathering. It stated that British-American invasion armies were assembling on the Kent and Cornwall coasts for the decisive battles of the war and General Eisenhower was putting the final touches to the gigantic plan that would in the near future be brought into action, according to a Paris broadcast on the previous day.

'German U-boats,' the announcer added, 'are on the alert in the English Channel ready to pounce on the invasion fleet.

'Along the whole of Europe's coastline, German soldiers are waiting for zero hour. Tanks, artillery of every calibre, flame throwers and machine-guns are waiting on the beaches to repel the invaders.'

German Radio stated: 'Contrary to 1918, the American troops will confront a German army unshaken in its fighting spirit – an army whose heart is not weakened by the home front, but inspired by iron determination and a tremendous lust for reprisal.'

The Paris correspondent of the Madrid ABC also reported that Rommel has been appointed chief of army operations for the second front, with headquarters in France, under the orders of Von Rundstedt.

A poster supporting the 'Salute a Soldier' campaign. Their slogan was, 'Save more, lend more.'

During February, 169 American aircraft arrived at RAF St Mawgan. The base had been built between 1942 and 1943 to extend the RAF Trebelzue airfield which had proven too small. The main runway had been extended in the early part of 1944.

The *Western Morning News* of Tuesday, 8 February reported on the Salute the Soldier campaign. It stated that at the annual meeting of Camborne, Redruth and Stithians National Savings Committee, a date was provisionally fixed for the week commencing Saturday, 3 June for the campaign to commence and placed the target at £250,000.

Miss F. Dyer, the honorary secretary, reported that there were 221 savings groups – an increase of six. Two selling centres opened at

Camborne and Redruth and were much appreciated, particularly by group secretaries.

During 1944, HMS Vulture II, a satellite of RNAS St Merryn, was laid out with imitation tanks, a bridge, road convoy and a landing strip to represent a Japanese-occupied area. These were to be used for training exercises. The air-to-ground and air-to-sea bombing and gunnery range was located at Treligga, which was west of Delabole.

The *Western Morning News* of Saturday, 12 February carried a story about the book drive. It read:

> There were people in Cornwall who when the Lord-Lieutenant suggested a target of 600,000 books for the county book drive thought the figure rather high. Full result of the drive is not yet known, but already over a million books of various kinds have been harvested, thanks to no small degree to Cornish children and to members of the indefatigable WVS.
>
> I have no doubt that the scrutineers have done their job thoroughly and that the books will go to the most appropriate destinations.
>
> If the county does as well in the forthcoming 'Salute the Soldier' savings drive, everybody concerned should be highly gratified.
>
> In the three major campaigns for savings held since the war started, Cornwall has put up a total of over nine million pounds. Even at this stage of the war, when the result must mainly depend upon the patriotism and thrift of small savers, there is no reason why another three million should not be added.
>
> Stirring events ahead will doubtless provide a stimulus to this campaign which nothing else could do quite so potently. The proper supplement to this, it seems to me, is the wise and generous use of Cornish speakers, who from their own distinguished service in the army and their local knowledge and experience, can best act as links between the soldier and those called upon in this campaign to salute him.

Flower smuggling was mentioned in the same day's newspaper. It mentioned that in Cornwall and the Isles of Scilly, the spring flowers bloom in winter and were a source of aesthetic delight and the basis of a sizable industry, especially in peacetime.

When the transport ban was put in place during the previous year, a much older industry made a reappearance in a form that would have made it unrecognizable to the old captains of the industry. This was the smuggling of flowers to the London markets which, if it produced rich rewards in the Metropolis, resulted also in a crop of not insignificant penalties in the Cornish courts.

Apparently, there was disquiet at Whitehall at a rumoured recrudescence of 'flower running' and Cornwall's name was linked with the traffic once more, as well as that of the Isles of Scilly.

In Cornwall, there were no transport obstacles to growers, who could send to market freely all the flowers they wished to dispose of from their severely restricted acreage.

The *Western Morning News* of Monday, 21 February reported that the Salute the Soldier Campaign had opened in Cornwall. It stated that Lord Kindersley, President of the National Savings Movement, on the previous Saturday, inaugurated the Cornwall 'Salute the Soldier' campaign at a crowded gathering at the Moresk Drillhall, Truro.

The Lord-Lieutenant, who presided, said that good as Cornwall had done they must do better still or be ashamed of themselves.

Lord Kindersley said he had no illusions as to who was responsible for the success of the savings movement. 'It is you and other workers like you throughout the country,' he said.

In the 'Wings for Victory' campaign, Cornwall showed an increase over the Warship Week effort of nearly £1,100,000, of which £700,000 represented an increase in small savings. It was an improvement of which they could be justly proud.

He had come there to ask them once again to break their already good record, as he believed the country as a whole would do. He was sure they could do it if their organization was as complete as possible in every detail.

The *Evening Despatch* of Thursday, 2 March reported that a

Black American troops at Grampound Road near Truro during March 1944. Troops were segregated to stop them fighting with each other. The black GIs mixed happily with the people of Cornwall, including the women, which angered some of the white GIs.

Personnel of the 329th Harbour Craft Company assembling barges from prefabricated units during March 1944. The work took place on the Cornish side of the Hamoaze in preparation of the D Day landings on 6 June.

sentence of imprisonment for life had been passed at a United States Court Martial in south-east England on a black American soldier, Private Joseph Bellot, aged 21, for an assault on a 16-year-old girl.

The court sat from 1 o'clock in the afternoon until 2 the following day. Bellot pleaded not guilty.

The sentence was subject to confirmation by the US Army Reviewing Authority.

On 18 March, a Consolidated USAAF B24D crashed at Pennatillie Farm near St Columb Major. The plane had left RAF St Mawgan during the early hours of the morning. The five crewman were killed and the plane was completely burnt out.

On 11 April, 111 anti-personnel and ten phosphorous bombs fell on fields at Menheniot near Liskeard.

During the spring of 1944, accommodation was sought for the

Brigadier J.W. Pendelbury takes the salute during the opening of the 'Salute the Soldier' campaign in Liskeard during April 1944. The Royal Marine 'Wrens' can be seen marching past the saluting base.

many troops based in the south west who were preparing for the D Day landings. Thousands of temporary camps were erected.

Bell tents were set up in various camps located at Truro, Chacewater and Wheal Busy. The 29th Division of the United States Army were housed at the Wheal Busy camps before heading off to the beaches of Utah and Omaha in Normandy.

The *Coventry Evening Telegraph* of Thursday, 20 April reported on a double tragedy in Cornwall. It stated that the deaths of a Land Girl and a young man, who was found shot after a 'Salute the Soldier' dance, would be investigated at Liskeard, Cornwall, on the following day.

Liskeard and district was celebrating its 'Salute' week and, on the Tuesday evening, there was a dance at the little hamlet of Rilla Mill. It was attended by a party of young people, including Raymond Bartlett (26), of Trebear Farm, North Hill, and the land girl, Miss Joyce Recover (21), a native of Kingston, Surrey, who for the past two years had been employed as a timber feller on the Trebartha estate. After the dance, Miss Recover did not return to her lodgings, and the manager of the timber works made inquiries of Bartlett's employer. Bartlett was found in bed and was questioned about the girl's whereabouts and was told to join in the search to find her. Soon afterwards, a shot was heard and Bartlett was found dead in bed.

The search was then continued for the girl and she was found dead in a cowshed near the dance hall.

The *Lincolnshire Echo* of Tuesday, 2 May reported that the Royal National Lifeboat Institution had made rewards of 14 guineas to the crew of its lifeboat at Newquay, Cornwall, who went out in a fog to an aeroplane which had crashed. They brought in twelve bodies, mail bags and £45,000 in 100-dollar bills.

The *Western Morning News* of Thursday, 11 May carried a story about Cornwall having women police. The Standing Joint Committee, meeting at Bodmin, on the previous day, decided to augment the Women's Auxiliary Police Corps in the county by the temporary appointment of twenty attested auxiliary policewomen.

The Special Committee appointed to consider the matter reported that they had given careful consideration to the letter from the Secretary of State on the question of employment of policewomen, and in this connection had had the advantage of conferring with Major Egan, one of his Majesty's inspectors of constabulary on the problem. After very careful and prolonged consideration of all the circumstances, they recommended that in the light of the terms of the letter of the Secretary of State, the Women's Auxiliary Police Corps in the county be augmented by the temporary appointment of a suitable number of attested auxiliary policewomen.

On the night of 30 May, Falmouth suffered during one of the worst air raids on Cornwall.

American troops leaving from Barn Pool on the Mount Edgcumbe Estate, heading for the beaches of Normandy during June 1944.

American troops landing on the shores of Normandy during D Day.

American troops loading Jeeps and equipment as they prepare to leave Barn Pool at Mount Edgcumbe for D Day.

The mass exodus of troops leaving for D Day. Many barrage balloons can be seen flying in the skies above the men.

During June 1944, thousands of American troops complete with armour, equipment and supplies left from ports in Cornwall for the battlefields of northern France. Embarkation points were located in and around Falmouth, at Trebah in the Helford Estuary and at Barn Pool on the Mount Edgcumbe Estate.

Operation Overlord (D Day) commenced on 6 June 1944. Over

US troops leaving for D Day. The hills of Cornwall can be seen in the background.

Brigadier J.W. Pendelbury again receives the salute during the opening of the 'Salute the Soldier' campaign, this time in St Austell in June 1944. The saluting base was in front of the parish church.

130,000 men left for the shores of Northern France and were followed soon after by many more. The success of the operation led to the end of the Second World War.

The *Hull Daily Mail* of Monday, 12 June reported that in the flower fields of Cornwall, three weeks ahead of the normal season, 30,000 tons of new potatoes were replacing the loss of the Channel Islands crops.

The *Cornishman* of Thursday, 15 June carried a story about a disturbance in Cornwall. It stated that in a fracas in Causewayhead, Penzance, between American sailors on the previous Monday night, Mr T. Watkins (52), of 22, Taroveor Terrace, Penzance, who was walking home with his wife at about 10.15, was knocked down and had to be removed to the West Cornwall Hospital.

A crowd quickly gathered on the spot and the sailors were marched away under an armed escort. Mr Watkins, who was employed on the Penzance quay, was reported to be progressing favourably, though it was not known whether he had suffered any severe injury.

The *Western Morning News* of Thursday, 29 June carried a story of two brothers who had drowned. It told that there was a double fatality off Cape Cornwall on the previous Tuesday evening. Two brothers, Henry Hocking, of Cape Cornwall Road, St Just and Pascoe Hocking, of Princess Street, St Just, both miners, went out on a small boat and when they were between the Brissons and Cape Cornwall, where there was always a very strong tide running, got into difficulty. Their situation was observed by the coastguard at Sennen, who called out the Sennen lifeboat for their assistance. The lifeboat, however, on reaching the scene, was unable to find any trace of the boat or the occupants. The bodies had not been recovered.

The *Western Morning News* of Tuesday, 11 July reported that there were no suitable women for Cornwall's police force. It said that the subject of women police was again mentioned at the meeting of Cornwall Standing Joint Committee at Bodmin on the previous day when the chief constable (Major E. Hare) reported that advertisements had been inserted in the local newspapers and the police press for police women.

Suitable candidates had not yet been forthcoming but applications were still being received. Four ex-members of the WAAF had been allocated by the Secretary of State to Cornwall and these were undergoing training.

Bude-Stratton Urban Council had passed a resolution welcoming the appointment of women police and requesting that one or more should be allocated to the Council's area and a further resolution had been received from Stratton Women's Institute also welcoming the appointment of women police for Cornwall and requesting that one or more should be allocated to that part of North Cornwall.

The letter stated that the members of the institute felt very strongly for the need for proper supervision of young women who in these times apparently could not look after themselves.

The *Coventry Evening Telegraph* of Tuesday, 11 July stated that Sir James Griggs, Secretary for War, had announced in the Commons that the government had decided to raise the ban on access to areas in Cornwall, Devon, Dorset and a part of Hampshire consisting of Bournemouth, Christchurch and the rural district of Ringwood and Fordingbridge, as from the following morning. Sir James, replying to Mr Strauss, said that the government had considered whether any relaxation of the orders governing the present protected areas was possible in order to allow persons from other parts of Southern England to enter those areas. For operational reasons the ban on access to the rest of the areas originally scheduled had to be maintained but the government had decided that permission to enter the areas should be extended to persons evacuated from London and certain other evacuable areas of Southern England, namely unaccompanied schoolchildren, mothers of children under five and expectant mothers and secondly under private arrangement by persons holding certificates issued by local authorities in the evacuable areas. The private arrangements covered, in addition to the above categories, mothers of children of school age, the infirm, the invalid, aged and blind persons.

On 20 July, a Sportsman's Day was held at Callington in connection with the 'Salute the Soldier' Week. An evening cricket match was the main attraction. At midday, the next day, a large crowd gathered in Fore Street where an old cricketer and footballer, Mr W.S. Rogers, the district secretary, announced the amount raised was more than twice that raised by their challengers, Camelford, with each target being £75,000.

The Lord Lieutenant of Cornwall, together with the mayor of Penzance, taking the salute during the march-past at the opening of the Penzance 'Salute the Soldier' campaign in July 1944.

The *Portsmouth Evening News* of Saturday, 22 July carried a story about the hard work of a boy farmer. It stated that while he was ill in bed recently, the whole of Mr Harold Martin's farm at Callington, Cornwall, was ploughed single-handed by his 12-year-old son, who did running repairs to the tractor and also helped on neighbour's fields, all after school hours.

The *Western Morning News* of Thursday, 17 August carried a story about air raid shelters. It reported that Lieutenant-Colonel E.H.W. Bolitho, the chairman of the Emergency Committee of Cornwall County Council, wrote:

> We are pleased to know how well things are going in Normandy and Brittany. The risk incurred by householders were they to give up their Morrison shelter is almost negligible. It is far outweighed by the needs of areas suffering constant enemy attack. May I, through your paper, appeal to householders to return their Morrison shelters to the authorities from whom they received them so that Cornwall can assist London in its hour of trial? If there is a wish that the shelter should be returned, it will be replaced in the course of a few weeks, as new shelters are now being constructed in large numbers.

The *Western Morning News* of Monday, 21 August told how Cornwall had helped with parcels of food for Prisoners of War. The report mentioned that the second year of the Cornwall Prisoners of War Food Parcel Fund commenced on 1 April, and since that date the following amounts had been forwarded to the Duke of Gloucester's Fund: April £1,069 7s 3d, May £1,262 9s 2d, June £1,391 0s 6d and July £2,861 15s 6d, making a total of £6,584 12s 5d.

The figure showed that Cornwall was well on its way to reaching its target of £19,604 which is needed to reimburse the Duke of Gloucester's fund for the cost of feeding prisoners from the county. The sum was in addition to moneys sent from Penny-a-Week, the Agriculture Fund and flag days and was due to individual enterprise and hard work and the activities of various committees and organizations throughout the county.

The *Cornishman* of Thursday, 31 August carried a story of Cornish hospitality. It told that Mr Donald W. Thomas, of Lowenac, Camborne, has received a letter from Colonel Butler B Miltonberger, of North Platte, Nebraska, the officer commanding the 134th Infantry Regiment of the United States Army, whom he met while the unit was in Cornwall. The letter read:

We all look back on our short stay in Cornwall as one of the highlights of the regiment's travels and I would appreciate it, if you care to, to have you extend our thanks to all Cornwall's good citizens for the many favours and the incomparable hospitality shown us while we were with you. We hope it has contributed to the further cementing of relations between our two nations.

The *Western Morning News* of Wednesday, 13 September mentioned Cornwall's first wrestling tournament since the beginning of the war. It stated that the first match was held at Helston on the previous Monday (Harvest Fair Day), under the auspices of the Cornwall Wrestling Association. The gate numbered about 1,300.

Welcoming the wrestlers and spectators, Mr Tregoning Hooper said that they wished the tournament to be a prelude to a successful revival of the sport in Cornwall after the war in its ancient vigour.

The opening ceremony was performed by Commander P.G. Agnew, MP, and Mrs Agnew, who were introduced by the mayor (Alderman

Rex Harrison in a scene from **Rakes Progress** *which was filmed in Cornwall during 1944. The film co-starred Lilli Palmer, a German actress and writer, who had married Harrison in 1943.*

J.H. Benney). Mrs Agnew distributed the prizes won at the baby show and dress parade.

The *Cornishman* of Thursday, 21 September carried an article about a touch of Hollywood in Cornwall. It told that the Gainsborough Film Company were making what they hoped would be one of their finest films.

To make the film, they had employed Rex Harrison (who had left for Totnes earlier in the week) and several other famous stars. Rex Harrison's understudy was a young, tall, fair-haired undergraduate who was on holiday in Cornwall and, because of his obvious interest, was now earning quite a substantial income to make a paying vacation.

The film was entitled *Rakes Progress*, and, it was stated, would probably be released by the following September. It was a French family film and it was hoped that it would cement international relationships.

Owing to the large influx of visitors to Cornwall at this time, several of the cast had to lodge at some distance from the location, a large number being at the White Hart Hotel at Hayle, while about a dozen were as far away as Penzance.

The *Western Morning News* of Friday, 22 September told the tale of a boy who had put poison in a cup of tea. It stated that, charged with attempting to poison his foster-mother by putting disinfectant in her tea, a boy of 12, resident at a Cornwall County Council Scattered Home, was at Liskeard Juvenile Court on the previous day, from where he was sent to a remand home, where he was to be psycho-analyzed.

Superintendent F. Sloman said that the boy had been in the home for some years, during which time the same foster-mother had been in charge. One of the boy's duties was to take tea to the foster-mother in the morning. On 10 August, the tea contained disinfectant.

The foster-mother was warned that she need not answer certain questions as a charge would probably be preferred against her. She said there were eight boys at the home and she had had to take disciplinary action on several occasions. She had punished the accused, who was very cruel to the other boys.

On 10 August, the boy brought tea to her bedside. It smelt strongly of disinfectant, so she did not drink it. She questioned him but he denied putting anything in the tea. She then asked him if he would drink the tea and he said 'Yes.' She poured out a cup and he drank it. After he had drunk the tea, he admitted putting disinfectant in it and she was alarmed and gave him some magnesia.

PS Miller read a statement made by the boy, which was alleged to have stated that he had had 'so much stick from mother that he got to dislike her.' There were maggots in their broth and the mother told them to take out the maggots and eat the broth. He did so but he made up his mind to pay her out for it. After he had taken the mother the tea, in which he had put two tablespoonfuls of disinfectant, he came downstairs. She made him drink a cup of it, saying he wouldn't get breakfast until he did.

The boy had been in scattered homes pretty well all of his life and did not know his father or mother, said Superintendent Sloman.

The *Cornishman* of Thursday, 28 September printed a letter of thanks from American troops to the people of Cornwall. It read:

Somewhere in France.

Sept. 12 1944.

Dear Friends,

Before the invasion, a large group of American soldiers spent many pleasant days in Cornwall and in Penzance in particular. The people of Cornwall took these soldiers into their homes and into their hearts. Penzance and the surrounding towns became a home away from home to these men and, like myself, they will look forward to the time when this war will end and they will be able to return to the States via Cornwall. I have served as a doctor on the battlefield to many of these 'Cornish Yanks' since the first day of the invasion.

We often speak of your country and of our hopes to visit it again. A wound which necessitates treatment back in England is often considered a blessing to many battle weary soldiers because it may afford them the opportunity to visit their friends in Cornwall again. No doubt many of our wounded have returned to you for that short visit which their only pass from the hospital will permit them before they are returned to the Continent to enter into the combat again. Many a wounded soldier's eyes light up and he bears his pain with a bit more ease when I tell him that he'll be all right, that his wound is his ticket to that pass to Cornwall. They often look up and ask, 'Do you really think I'll make it, Doc? Do you think I'll get to go back there again?' Cornwall is a second home to those veterans among us who remain. We have many new faces among us who know nothing of the kind Cornish countryside and its good people and who probably have some difficulty in understanding our affection for them. We speak of you often and look forward to the day when we can be home in Cornwall again.

Sincerely yours,

(Dr.) ALFRED M. TOCKER. Capt., M.C., U.S. Army.

The *Western Morning News* of Monday, 30 October carried news of the trial of a lorry driver accused of causing the death of a Land Girl.

It stated that a jury at Cornwall Assize at Bodmin on the previous Saturday found William Kenneth Thomas. 39, lorry driver 'Not guilty' of the manslaughter of Peggy Josephine Mill, a Land Girl, at Helston Road. Roseudgeon, Perranuthnoe on 3 July.

The charge arose from a road accident. The jury also found him 'Not Guilty' of driving a lorry in a manner dangerous to the public Discharging the prisoner, Mr Justice Mcnaghten said he hoped that the case would have shown him and others what a responsible thing it was to drive a motor vehicle over a public road and that no care could be too great to prevent an accident.

RAF St Mawgan was used by the 8th Air Force and the RAF for large-scale bomber diversions during the winter of 1944 until the beginning of 1945.

The *Western Morning News* reported on 6 November that 40 per cent of the 198 fires reported to the NFS in No 19 Fire Force Area, which covered south-west Devon and Cornwall, were down to carelessness. A quarter of these, statistics revealed, were caused by dropped cigarettes and matches while another quarter were due to unattended rubbish fires. Other causes included children playing with matches and electrical faults.

The *Cornishman* of Thursday, 9 November reported on coal in Cornwall. It mentioned that Captain N.A. Beechman, MC, Member of Parliament for the St Ives Division, had received a letter from Major G. Lloyd George (Minister of Fuel and Power), about stocks of coal at the West Cornwall ports, with particular reference to Porthleven. This was in reply to a letter from Captain Beechman.

'Information available,' wrote Major Lloyd George, 'showed that the total stock at those ports and at the depots, dependent on seaborne supplies, amounted to several weeks' supply in terms of the present allocations.'

This showed that in spite of the shortage of small boats, supplies had been well maintained and that the position in West Cornwall generally need not cause anxiety except at Porthleven and at Helston. But at Porthleven, the stocks at 30 September amounted to less than one week's supply; and at Helston to less than two weeks. The position was being carefully watched and if it was not possible to provide the necessary tonnage by sea, action would have to be taken to make up the deficiency by forwarding supplies by rail to Nancegollan.

The *Cornishman* of Thursday, 30 November told of a youth rally in Cornwall. It reported that an 'All Canadian' Youth Rally, the first of its kind to take place in Cornwall, was held at St Ives during the previous week-end. It was sponsored by the St Ives Girls' Training Corps and Youth Club and various representatives and leaders of Youth Clubs in the West attended. The programme consisted of Ministry of Information films, talks and discussions, all of which were about Canada and Canadian life. The opening session on the Saturday afternoon was presided over by Mr W.C. Drage (Deputy Mayor of St Ives and a member of St Ives Youth Advisory Committee).

In the evening, the mayor (Mr W.J. Sullivan) extended an official welcome and a talk was given by Miss Diana Reader-Harris of the National Association of Girls' Clubs and Mixed Clubs. This was followed by a Canadian camp fire social. Canadian square dancing was organized by Miss E. Clarkson of the Central Council for Recreative Physical Training.

The Home Guard were officially stood down on 3 December although they were finally disbanded a year later. Each man received a certificate and those who had served more than 3 years received a Defence Medal. The Home Guard lost 1,206 members during the conflict due to rocket attacks and heavy bombing.

The *Cornishman* of Thursday, 7 December reported on the blackout in Cornwall. It stated that Lieutenant-Colonel E.H.W. Bolitho, the chairman of the County Council, had received a letter from the Minister of Home Security, stating that the position of the black-out in Cornwall was under review. Colonel Bolitho wrote to the Minister as a result of a Resolution requesting him to do so, passed by the County Council on November 14.

A farewell meeting of a group of the Home Guard at Longlands, Saltash during 1944.

Evacuees from Epsom and Ewell being escorted by Inspector J.H. Tucker at Wadebridge station during June 1944. A Doodlebug had fallen at Ewell on 16 June and the bombing of the area got so bad that children no longer attended school. It was decided to evacuate many to Cornwall.

The *Western Morning News* of Saturday, 16 December told of evacuee children returning home. It reported that children attending Tamar Central School, which had been evacuated to Truro, would be home for Christmas and would remain in Plymouth, sharing for their school building the Junior Technical School.

The deaf school was also returning from South Brent to Hartley House. Mr E.S. Leatherby, chairman of Plymouth Education Committee, told the *Western Morning News* that only those children who had homes in the city would return to Plymouth. The others would be able to stay in the rural areas by arrangement with the Devon and Cornwall County authorities.

Mr Leatherby said that the school children would be having their Christmas parties and gifts distributed to them from the Lord Mayor of London's Fund. Children away from Plymouth would also be given help towards their Christmas parties. 'The education department have the interest of all the children at heart and everything in their power to give them a happy Christmas will be done.'

The *Gloucester Citizen* of Wednesday, 27 December reported that Cornwall was celebrating as the blackout was lifted. It mentioned that relaxation of black-out restrictions in Cornwall for all but a few coastal areas had taken the county by surprise and some people could not believe the news. Until the previous Saturday, all of Cornwall, except Launceston and the adjoining parishes, had maintained a complete black-out. In celebration, town bands played in the streets and there was more organized carol singing than there had been since 1939.

The *Cornishman* of Thursday, 28 December told of a visit by Father Christmas. It stated that members of Penzance High Street Methodist Church crowned a very busy December by a very fine series of efforts over Christmas, as a result of which a number of people were given gifts and good cheer. Four large Christmas trees were placed in the church, the gift of Lieutenant-Colonel E.H.W. Bolitho. They were put in position by Mr W.H. Green. Services began on the Sunday morning, when the preacher was Mr E.G. James, and the choir gave the anthem 'Hark, the glad sound.' This and all other services were very well attended.

The children's Christmas tree service was held on the Sunday afternoon, conducted by the minister (Reverend W.V. Sibson). Nurses from the West Cornwall Hospital were stationed at two of the trees to receive the children's gifts. They were assisted by Messrs Howard Tonkin and Philip Uren, two members of the church home on leave from the Forces.

A short musical programme was given, arranged by Miss Grose, in which Jennifer Lawry and Maureen Polkinghorne gave solo items, other pieces being given by the primary and junior Sunday schools. Lester Bolitho was at the organ.

During the service, a surprise visit was paid by the mayor of Penzance (Alderman Robert Thomas), who gave a brief talk to the children.

By the end of the evening service, over three hundred gifts had been collected. Old and young alike went up to the trees and handed their presents to the nurses, who were at this time on duty at all four of the trees. Many gifts were also left by people who were away from the town for Christmas.

Mr Sibson conducted the service, the theme of which was the story of the Nativity in lesson and song.

During the offering of the gifts, selections were given by the organist (Mr R.W. Whatley), whose playing at all services added greatly to their attraction.

Carols were sung by the choir and Miss Elise Harvey of St Buryan sang 'Rest,' 'The Holy City' and 'Bless this House.' She delighted the large congregation, who found her last number especially inspiring, sung as it was with the trees lit by special lamps which also flood-lit the Communion Table.

After a short service on Christmas morning, in which the choir gave the carol, 'In the Bleak Midwinter,' the trees were stripped and the vast array of gifts sorted into their various groups before being taken to the West Cornwall Hospital in the afternoon.

The visit to the hospital was the highlight of the whole Christmas. Father Christmas was there on a sleigh drawn by five angels (Betty Weekes, Maureen Polkinghorne, Ruth Harvey, Marjorie Carn and Jacqueline Carpenter) and an attractive picture it made as it was driven into the various wards.

Father Christmas himself gave presents to all the children, whilst he was assisted in the women's ward by Messrs Jenkin and Malone, and in the men's ward by Mesdames Harvey and Gowith. No one was forgotten and the sleigh was even transported upstairs on the lift. Carols were sung, accompanied by Mr J.H. Martin on his accordion and altogether the visit was one which would not readily be forgotten either by the patients or by the visitors.

In the afternoon, Mr Sibson, together with Messrs E.J. Hutchens and W. Foss (both of whom played a large part in the success of the Christmas programme) paid a visit to Madron Institution, where gifts were distributed.

Other Yuletide activities were the sending of special gifts to members of the church away ill at Tehidy; the sending of 7s 6d to every member of the church away on service; and the singing of carols around the town on behalf of the National Children's Home and Orphanage.

One and all, from the youngest child to the oldest member of the church, co-operated to ensure that Christmas, 1944, would be an unforgettable one in the annuals of Penzance High Street Methodist Church.

CHAPTER SEVEN

1945 – Victory

During 1945, RAF Cleave closed. It had been operational since 1939. RAF Davidstow Moor also closed in the same year along with RAF Perranporth.

The *Cornishman* of Thursday, 4 January told how wounded soldiers were entertained by children at Penzance. It mentioned that on Boxing Day, patients at the West Cornwall Hospital, Penzance, were given a charming entertainment by a group of children, assisted by Nurse Payne, who had a lovely voice, and Mr H. Manning, a wizard on his harmonica.

Mr Gordon Casey, who was still a patient at the hospital arranged the show which was varied and colourful.

The children taking part were Pauline Batten, Elizabeth Jose, Barbara Lambert, Edith Mooney, Sally Scrase and Douglas Williams. The show was compered by Mr Ballard.

On Wednesday, Mrs H.O. Scrase arranged a show for the Trewiddon Convalescent Home. The children were given a most enthusiastic welcome by the staff and patients. The majority of the soldiers convalescing there were married men with children of their own and they were obviously moved by the talent the children displayed.

Little Pauline Batten made a great hit, both by her splendid elocution and her winsome manner, whilst Elizabeth Jose won the admiration of all in the dignified yet youthful manner in which she recited her choice little poems. Sally Scrase seemed to know just what the troops wanted and in 'Swinging on a Star' and 'Chocolate Soldier from the USA,' she had them with her in spirit and voice from start to finish.

Edith Mooney and Barbara Lambert in national dances were a delight to watch and received a great ovation.

Douglas Williams sang some stirring songs with great sincerity and, as far as the patients were concerned, could have gone on singing all night.

Mr C. Ballard ably compered the show and also sang some humorous songs which were very popular. After the concert, the staff, under their Commandant (Miss Sturmer), entertained the children in the beautifully decorated hall where a wonderful Christmas tree stood. There were gifts on the tree for all and no effort was spared to show their appreciation of the entertainment.

On the Friday, the same programme was given at St Michael's Hospital, Hayle. Again, a warm welcome awaited the party and a great reception was given to each artiste. A welcome addition to the programme was made by Miss Doreen Williams, her 'Alice Blue Gown' being one of the popular numbers of the evening.

The good sisters were full of gratitude and saw that the children were refreshed with warm drinks and a light meal before their journey home. Mrs Jordan, worked hard at the evacuee concerts as their pianist and the gratitude of everyone went to her for her helpfulness.

The *Cornishman* of Thursday, 18 January told of a booklet for US troops. It stated that an interesting and informative little booklet had been compiled for members of the United States Armed Forces, serving in the United Kingdom, as a guide which would help them during visits to the county. It was called 'West Cornwall' and carried a foreword by Lieutenant Colonel E.H. W. Bolitho. Containing descriptions of many of the beauty spots and historical sites and buildings, it had details of Truro, Falmouth, Helston, The Lizard, Camborne, Redruth, Penzance, the Isles of Scilly, St Ives and Newquay, together with full information regarding accommodation, canteens, amusements, sports, travel, etc.

During February, the National Fire Service in Cornwall and South-West Devon was called out to fifty-eight non-enemy fires. Official figures showed that carelessness was responsible for twenty-one of this total. Unextinguished cigarette ends and matches caused two outbreaks, while unattended rubbish fires and electrical faults accounted for another three fires each. There were also thirteen outbreaks, the causes of which varied but suggested carelessness.

The *Western Morning News* of Friday, 16 February reported that Lady Vivian, the county organizer, while at Truro, gave an interesting review of the work done by the WVS in Cornwall during the past year. There were, she said, 12,357 members of the organization in Cornwall.

The work of the year had been in two divisions – before and after D Day. 'A tremendous amount of preparation went on before D Day,' she said. The WVS did an immense amount of training for the rest centres. In preparation for D Day, they had six mobile canteens; they had liaison officers in each town and they had seventeen clothing dumps and thirteen clothing depots.

They arranged for emergency cooking for the Home Guard, if called into action. They arranged for sixty mobile squads who were on call if need be and she felt that the arrangements made by Mr S.W. King, the Public Assistance officer, were splendid and they owed him a great debt of gratitude.

One of the most interesting things that happened before D Day was the growth of the British Welcome Clubs, of which they had twenty working for a short while. It was a tremendous relief that their organization was not called into operation.

Then there was the problem of evacuation again, and between 15,000 and 16,000 evacuees arrived in Cornwall, over 6,000 of whom passed through the rest centres. They had 100 centres for their reception and eighteen local authority areas were affected.

In the latter half of the year, they had a great deal of routine work and had four mobile canteens doing rounds and eleven static canteens. The contributions from these to the Regional Trust were £1,240. They served over 1,000,000 meals, nearly 1,500,000 beverages and 1,500,000 cigarettes.

They had been asked to do new work, including overseas knitting for liberated countries. They had returned over 2,500 garments, over 60 per cent of their quota, which was quite good. There had been the working parties for the CHSS clothing exchanges, National Savings, a flag day (which raised £1,800 for army welfare) and the volunteer car pool, in which 754,147 miles were recorded.

The Regional Commissioner had been extraordinarily helpful to the WVS. He was resigning and she proposed that they should send a message of thanks to him for what he had done for them. This was agreed to. Lady Vivian expressed thanks also to the county secretary

(Mrs Marshall) and her assistant (Mrs Radmore), the training officers, Mrs Phillips (the clothing officer) and her deputy (Mrs Henry), Mrs Britton and Mrs Bennett in the evacuee departments, and Miss Smith, for the Assistance Board and Soldiers and Sailors' Families' Association work.

They had now sent 6,000 articles of clothing overseas and had another demand for a further 7,000.

Mr G.H. Johnstone, county ARP controller, said the record of the WVS was a proud one and he could not have done his job at all but for their help and co-operation.

Cornwall had adopted Battersea. Wandsworth and Lambeth under the homing scheme and collections were being made in the county to try and rehome some of the people bombed out of their homes.

By March 1945, the film going public could buy ice cream again. It had been withdrawn from Gaumont cinemas in 1942.

The *Derby Daily Telegraph* of Thursday, 22 March carried a story about roses from Cornwall. It noted that flowers from the West of England were arriving in great quantities. During the week, 15,000 boxes had been conveyed by the GWR, including roses and carnations from Cornwall to Covent Garden.

Golden daffodils at Marazion during February 1945. Early spring flowers in the county were rare due to the lack of fuel available needed to heat greenhouses. However, sunshine had brought along many early daffodils.

The *Western Times* of Thursday, 29 March published a story about fears of unemployment in the region. It stated that there was fear that widespread unemployment would await ex-Servicemen returning to Cornwall after the war. The South-Western Federation of Trades Councils held their annual meeting at the University College, Gandy Street in Exeter and passed a resolution that:

This group of trades Councils views with alarm the remote prospects of full post-war employment for the mass of workers in the more industrial areas of Cornwall and desires that Cornwall shall be scheduled as a development area to enable the Duchy to play its full part in the rebuilding of Britain after the war.

In early April, the Allies pushed into Italy and Western Germany while the Soviet and Polish forces stormed Berlin at the end of the month.

The *Western Morning News* of Friday, 27 April reported on evacuees in Cornwall. It mentioned that the government evacuation scheme for the welfare of unaccompanied children was discussed on the previous day at Truro, a conference held under the auspices of Cornwall County Council. Mr A. Browning Lyne, chairman of the Education Committee, who presided, said remarkable success had been achieved in regard to evacuation and paid tribute to the way in which they had backed the demand of the Ministerial departments. Miss Faithful, regional welfare officer, speaking of the welfare of unaccompanied children and the supervision of billets, said from the beginning it had been the Minister's policy that unaccompanied children should be well supervised and that welfare services must be maintained until every child returned. Soon, they hoped unaccompanied children and other evacuees could return, and it would be a difficult time, especially for the children who would be left behind. These would require complete supervision until they too, returned.

Children in Cornwall had been exceedingly happy and a lot of them had done very well, added the speaker. Many would be sorry to see the evacuees go home.

Miss Faithful said in regard to those whose homes were destroyed, there were only eighty cases from Plymouth who had not been able to return home. She did not know the size of the London problem.

Mr S.P. Heath, education secretary, spoke of a county register of billets, suitable for use as foster homes, and said they would be glad of the names of good homes. The education authority had accepted responsibility for eighty children.

Mr J.E. Dodwell, the Ministry of Health evacuation officer, dealt with the residual problem consequent on the return home of evacuees, urging that co-ordinated arrangements were necessary and that they could not deal with an undisciplined return of mothers and children. He outlined these arrangements.

On 28 April, Benito Mussolini was killed by Italian partisans. German forces surrendered in Italy on the following day. On 30 April, Adolf Hitler committed suicide in his bunker in Berlin. The news

On 28 April 1945, Benito Mussolini was killed by Italian partisans.

The Queen on a Victory visit to Stepney on 9 May.

reached Cornwall two days later. Many people thought that the story was a hoax.

With the capture of the Reichstag, the military defeat of Nazi Germany was signalled.

Germany surrendered unconditionally on 7 May to much jubilation all over the world.

Victory in Europe Day fell on 8 May and the official ceasefire ended a minute after midnight on 9 May. Huge celebrations took place all over Cornwall with every city, town and village organising its own parades and street parties with endless flags and bunting as well as bonfires and firework displays. Most bonfires featured an effigy of Hitler on top. For the first time since the beginning of the war, shops once more lit up their windows.

The Admiralty lifted lighting restrictions in coastal areas on 11 May and normal street lighting returned and traffic lights no longer had to be masked.

The *Western Morning News* of Friday, 11 May reported that the king had thanked Cornwall. It mentioned that Lieutenant-Colonel E.H.W. Bolitho had received a telegram from His Majesty the King in reply to the congratulatory telegram sent to him in the name of the county of Cornwall. It read: 'I thank you sincerely for the loyal terms in which you have conveyed to me the congratulations of the people of Cornwall on the victorious conclusion of the war against Germany.'

The *Western Morning News* of Tuesday, 15 May reported on prisoners of war. It noted that Lieutenant-Colonel E.H.W. Bolitho, the

Children on the Treneere Estate in Penzance enjoying a Victory tea. Fire parties, ARP Wardens and others joined together to prepare the event. A fancy dress parade also took place.

Children follow a man with a barrel organ at Victory celebration on a Penzance estate.

Lord-Lieutenant, presiding at a meeting of Cornwall Territorial Army Association at Truro, on the previous, day had stated: 'We may rest assured that the interests of repatriated prisoners of war coming back to our county are being well looked after in every way.' He said that many men were coming back and the last thing they wished was to impose on charity in any shape or form. In many cases, however, they were in straitened circumstances and it was only by interview that they could get them to say they wanted help.

Mr E.J. Hancock said some of the prisoners had been out of touch with home and people for so long that they had developed a peculiar type of mentality and every sympathy should be extended to them by the welfare officers, who should endeavour to see if special cases required attention.

The chairman said welfare officers in every area were informed of men who were returning, and it was their duty to see them personally and ascertain if they could do anything for them.

The Welfare Officer (Lieutenant-Colonel G.T. Williams) reported that there were only fifty-four canteens and eight mobile canteens now in operation in the county. The hostel at Redruth continued to carry out excellent work and it was felt that more hostels in Cornwall could be very usefully employed if allowed.

This especially applied to seaside places such as Falmouth,

Newquay, Penzance and St Ives. These would be filled to the utmost in the summer months and in the winter they could be used, as at St Mawgan, for economic classes, etc.

Special attention had been given by welfare officers on the subject of agriculture. It provided occupation, especially on lonely sites, and it was welcomed by the services concerned. It provided fresh vegetables and free labour. As some thousands of demobilizing men and women were expected at some sites in the county, the need of occupation and amenities during the periods of waiting seemed obvious. Horticulture had been eagerly accepted on sites, especially by women.

The reservation of rooms in some of the principal towns for the use of service men and women who were stranded was continuing to prove of great value. In connection with the 'Get you home' scheme, drivers were now available to meet men at all the principal railway stations in Cornwall.

Mr Hancock said the association was much indebted to the welfare officer for all the work he had done with the support of Mrs Asher and Miss Lethbridge, to Mrs Maclaren for her work in connection with woollen comforts, and to Captain Rogers in connection with the entertainments of troops.

Although the war was over in Europe, fighting continued in Japan.

Children from Redinnick, together with the mayor, celebrating VE Day.

Cornish cadets taking part in a boxing match at Tregony during July 1945. All were members of the 3rd Cadet Battalion DCLI.

The spread for the children at St Mary's School playground in Penzance as part of the VE celebrations.

A VE party at Gwavas Street in Penzance.

A VE party for children at Chapel Street, Penzance.

Residents in New Street, Penzance celebrate Victory in Europe.

Another VE Day party at Penalverne Place, Penzance.

Land Girls picking potatoes in the Cornish countryside during July 1945.

On 6 August, the United States Army Air Forces dropped an atomic bomb on Hiroshima, Japan, which killed 80,000 people instantly. Nagasaki was bombed three days later, ultimately bringing the war in Japan to an end.

The *Cornishman* of Thursday, 9 August reported on the Cornwall Prisoner of War Parcel Fund. It stated that the Cornwall Prisoners of War Food Parcel Fund had come to an end on 30 June and since its inception in March, 1943. the magnificent sum of £45,544 1s 11d had been raised and forwarded to the Duke of Gloucester's Red Cross and St John Fund.

It was stated that Cornwall could be proud of the fact that, since March, 1943, the cost of the 10s weekly food parcel to each of Cornwall's prisoners of war in Europe had been met through the

Red Cross nurses marching in procession to Truro Cathedral at the County Civil Service stand-down parade in May 1945.

appeal. Mrs Eileen Beauchamp, county organizer, thanked all of the contributors.

The *Cornishman* of Thursday, 9 August reported that uranium deposits had been found in Cornwall. It noted that uranium, the heavy white metallic element found in the pitchblende, which was vital for the construction of the atomic bomb and to the release of atomic energy, was scattered fairly widely across the face of the earth from Cornwall to Norway, from North America to Russia and the Belgian Congo. There were also some sources in Saxony and Austria. The newspaper stated that Cornwall might well have a great part to play in the development of the marvellous, yet dreaded, discovery. Large quantities of uranium were reported to lie hidden in a hill near St Austell, while the county also contained much pitchblende, and it was estimated that eventually millions of horsepower might be generated from Cornish sources alone. Uranium had been found in rnines at St Just, Redruth and Grampound Road.

The marriage of Sub-Lieutenant Mare Andre Boiselair RCNVR to Wren Betty Payne of Falmouth during August 1945. Sub-Lieutenant Boiselair was Canadian by birth.

In 1942, derelict Cornish tin mines were re-opened with the help of Canadian miners, for Canada had taken a leading part in the development of the atomic bomb. A few years before the war, a French company worked the Terras Mine, 4 miles from St Austell on the road to Newquay, searching for radium, but the process proved uneconomic and the company went into liquidation. There were many mines such as Terras throughout the Duchy. Untold possibilities lay ahead for Cornwall, for the human race and for the world.

On 14 August, the new Prime Minister, Clement Attlee, announced the surrender of Japan. All over Cornwall, places of work were closed for two days during the VJ celebrations.

Miss Patricia Donnithorne of Penzance was crowned the borough's 'Victory Queen' during August 1945.

Miss Betty Goody, of 4 Church Street, Newlyn, who was the maid of honour to the Victory Queen.

Mrs Lillian Thomas of Barwis Hill, Penzance was the second maid of honour.

An effigy of Tojo (a general of the Imperial Japanese Army) was consumed by a huge bonfire lit by the mayor on Penzance promenade on VJ night.

A crowd of children at the Mennaye Fields, Penzance, watching a Punch and Judy show as part of a VJ programme prepared for them.

On 2 September, the Japanese surrender documents were signed on board the American battleship USS *Missouri*. This marked the official end of the Second World War.

With the war at an end, people celebrated but remembered their lost loved ones who had been killed on the battlefield. No family was

Douglas MacArthur signing the Japanese Instrument of Surrender on board the **Missouri** *in Tokyo Bay on 2 September 1945. The agreement formalized the surrender of Japan and brought the Second World War to an end.*

Truro Ambulance Cadets who were winners of the Trenhayle Cup at the first-aid competition in Hayle during August 1945. Shown are the St John Ambulance Cadet 'A' team.

The mayor and the corporation of Truro returning to the town hall after a service of celebration at the cathedral.

untouched by the war. Food remained rationed but people were now entitled to an extra half ounce of tea. However, rationing continued until 1954 and it was a long time before the county and the country recovered from its effects. The long process of rebuilding and returning to a normal way of life took place. Many cities were almost completely rebuilt and a way of life was lost forever.

The *Western Morning News* of Wednesday, 5 September debated the use of the atomic bomb. It noted that Commander Douglas Marshall, the MP for South-East Cornwall, speaking at Tywardreath on the previous night, gave a picture of the House of Commons as he saw it, and said he was disgusted at the singing of the 'Red Flag' at the opening of parliament. It seemed to him that a difference of opinion was far greater between the supporters of the government than between the government and the opposition. Referring to the atomic bomb, he thought the decision to use it was right. True, it was appalling but it stopped the tragedy of war and it was possible that the very frightfulness of it might prevent war. Everyone who had had a relative or friend fighting against Japan would say they did not want boys or men sacrificed a minute longer than could possibly be avoided.

As to the secret of the bomb, he thought that, until the World Security Council was set up and working with reasonable forces attached to it, it was right that America should go on holding the secret.

In regard to Lend-Lease, he urged that whatever happened it should not influence the friendship between the two races.

Speaking of demobilization, he said the hastening was not sufficient, although Mr Bevin's scheme was a fair one.

'We were going to go through a very hard time and the representatives of the Labour Party in the House of Commons were wondering when they were going to carry out the promises made in the election,' he stated.

Commander Marshall said that he intended to make his first speech on a bill or measure that assisted the division. The domestic side of the division was not political and his one aim and ambition was to help wherever he possibly could.

The *Western Morning News* of Thursday, 27 September carried a story under the headline 'Safe, Well, And Happy - Free from the Japs.' It stated that more men of the west had cabled home further good news. News of men released from the Japanese had been received by parents and relatives in Devon and Cornwall.

The Penzance Women's Voluntary Service was stood down during September 1945. They are pictured here at a social event to celebrate their past work.

Mr Donald Wickett, of Penarth, Cam Brea, received official intimation that both his father and mother (Mr and Mrs Fred Wickett), who had been prisoners in Japanese hands at Singapore for years, had been released. Mr Wickett had previously received news of the safety of his mother but no information was forthcoming as to his father.

With the surrender of Japan at the beginning of September, the war was truly over. However, its effects were to be felt for many years to come.

Acknowledgements

Thanks to Tina Cole, Alan Tait, Ellen Tait, Tilly Barker, Bruce Hunt and Steve Johnson. Thanks also to the helpful and friendly team at Pen and Sword, including Roni Wilkinson, Matt Jones, Jon Wilkinson, Irene Moore, Diane Wordsworth, Katie Eaton, Laura Lawton, Jodie Butterwood, Tara Moran and Lisa Goose.

Bibliography

Books:

Brown, Mike, *Put That Light Out!* (Sutton Publishing 1999)

Clamp, Arthur, *United States Naval Advanced Amphibious Base* (Arthur Clamp 1985)

Hancock, Peter, *Cornwall at War 1939-1945* (Halsgrove 2002)

Van der Kiste, John, *Plymouth: A City at War, 1914-1945* (History Press 2014)

Vosper, Douglas C., *Saltash Remembered Part 2* (Arthur Clamp 1981)

Vosper, Douglas C., *Saltash Remembered Part 3* (Arthur Clamp 1982)

Newspapers:

Cornishman

Coventry Evening Telegraph

Derby Daily Telegraph

Evening Dispatch

Gloucester Citizen

Hull Daily Mail

Lincolnshire Echo

Portsmouth Evening News

Sunday Mirror

Sunday Pictorial

West Briton and Cornwall Advertiser

Western Daily Press

Western Morning News

Western Times

Websites:

BBC People's War at www.bbc.co.uk/history/ww2peopleswar

Historical Cornwall at www.historic-cornwall.org.uk

Into Cornwall at www.intocornwall.com

Newquay Voice at www.newquayvoice.co.uk

Index